Ghosts Along the Erie

Ghosts Along the Erie

Mary Ann Johnson

North Country Books, Inc.
Utica, New York

GHOSTS ALONG THE ERIE

ISBN-10 0-925168-34-3
ISBN-13 978-0-925168-34-4

Second Printing 2007

Library of Congress Cataloging-in-Publication Data

Johnson, Mary Ann, 1923-
    Ghosts along the Erie / written by Mary Ann Johnson.
        p. cm.
    ISBN 0-925168-34-3
    1. Ghosts—New York (State)—Adirondack Mountains.
2. Ghost stories, American—New York (State)—Adirondack
Mountains. I. Title.
GR110.N7J64   1995
133.1'09747'5—dc20

9670

95-4165
CIP

North Country Books, Inc.
311 Turner Street
Utica, New York 13501
www.northcountrybooks.com

Dedicated to My Grandchildren

*Mark, Chris, Joseph, Michael,
Matthew, Megan, Kenzie and Jacqueline*

Acknowledgments

There are many people who contributed stories to this book of ghost legends and hauntings, and *Ghosts Along the Erie* would not have been possible without their help. I would like to thank the following families for their cooperation and contributions to this book and over the years: Abrams, Aldrich, Behm, Bernhardi, Blake-Hill, Belindo, Becca, Carner, Crandall, Colley, Ciricillo, Cook, Cooper, Emerson, France, Fischette, Guy, Giovanni, Howell, Harper, Humphrey, Irlando, Jetty, King, Klink, Kim, Littlefield, Longyear, Laporta, Lakota, Locastro, Leary, Leonard, McCarthy, McBride, Marr, Moore, Nicolosi, Purcell, Peel, Pleasant, Queirolo, Rooker, Rood, Riordans, Rabourn, Saverese, Sorrentino, Savey, Silcox, Tallcot, Tomenga, Thurston, Tallman, Vanek, VanDitto, and Vaughn. And thank you too, to those families who preferred not to be mentioned above.

—Mary Ann

Foreword

The towns spread out along the Erie Canal have a wealth of legends and folklore, and Port Byron, with its treasure-trove of ghost stories, is certainly no exception. Although these stories were undoubtedly embellished as they were passed down from generation to generation, many lifelong residents of the town believe they contain more than a modicum of truth. They can readily point out connections and coincidences that link these tales to long-dead residents of the town. Many of them are genuinely convinced that they themselves have seen apparitions, spirits and ghosts.

As I was growing up in Port Byron, I often heard stories of strange occurrences that had supposedly taken place there, and I discovered that some of my relatives and neighbors insisted that they, too, shared their homes with ghosts. Even my own grandparents believed they lived in a haunted house: "Who Snuffed Out the Candle" is about the frightening experiences they had while living there. Frankly, I was always skeptical, considering these tales to be the stuff of rumors and overactive imaginations, and I was intrigued that grownups had such strong fears about them. But eventually, so many reliable people (including my grandparents) reported such eerie happenings that I decided to check things out for myself. My love for legends, ghost stories, and folk tales, reinforced by my father's vast knowledge of local history, continues to be a hobby of mine to this very day.

Whether I believe in ghosts or not does not come into the picture as far as my writing about them is concerned. I try to investigate and study reports of these phenomena with an open mind, and I am impressed by the wealth of evidence I have discovered, as well as the strikingly similar reports from all over the country, going back to the beginning of its recorded history.

I have never had to turn down a story because a tale was too unbelievable or the storyteller unreliable. Still, I should caution the reader that these ghost stories are not history. They are legends of our area and as such, deserve to be preserved; whether they deserve to be believed is up to you.

This book tells of many Erie Canal sites where strange and bizarre phenomena have occurred. Some stories are a bit shady, a few are well known, while others are known to only the local townspeople. I've tried to cover them all: tales about the famous and not-so famous, haunted houses, locations of legends, and the reputed lairs of monsters and strange spirits.

For this book I have selected almost all of the famous ghost stories I came across during my five years of research. Many more exist that I didn't hear about until too late for this publication. Perhaps they'll be the subject of some future book.

I must emphasize that the inclusion of information about a haunted house does not mean that the house is open to the public. For reasons I am sure the reader will understand and respect, some names and exact locations have not been revealed. Area residents, however, will find that most of the stories and their locations are readily identifiable.

Rereading this book supposedly for the last time before sending it to the publisher, I was struck anew by how eerie this area can be after dark, when curious poltergeist manifestations occur almost nightly. But during the daylight hours, this delightful town and the surrounding ones make this a wonderful place for families to raise their children. I should know: seven generations of my family have called the area home.

It's worth going out of your way to visit this enchanting place. The towns stand today much as they were in the days of the horse and buggy. But men should be aware when they visit here. Legend has it that a female vampire is buried in a little graveyard at the edge of town and that her fatal beauty still lures men to this sinister spot when midnight comes around. But others in the area are convinced that these ghosts and haunted houses are as common and insignificant an annoyance as a barn full of mice—just that and nothing more!

Ghosts had fallen on hard times until recently, when ghost-busting movies and Stephen King's books suddenly began to entertain us in a scary way. Now I find more people enjoying scary incidents, and many have made an effort to report their eerie tales to me. I have collected over a hundred of their ghost stories since *Ghosts of Port Byron* was published in 1987, including some from children, who seem to enjoy writing them for school assignments and plays. It's clear that some of their stories are made up entirely, while others are hand-me-downs from their families.

Some say that ghosts have lost their glamour and power to terrify because so many people today accept their existence. What do you think? They still scare the daylights out of me!

Whenever I write a ghost story and I'm not getting it quite right, mysterious things start happening around me. My typewriter refuses to work, letters become blank on the paper, and important chapters disappear from my desktop. Now why would this happen? Is the spirit I'm writing about annoyed with the story and trying to get me to correct it? Several times I have double-checked with our historian, only to find out that I had been misinformed. Retyping the story was easy once the mistake was taken care of. At times these incidents upset me, but on the other hand, they are indications of real supernatural happenings taking place around us...if only we knew how to handle them.

It seems as if the spirits are intrigued that I am writing about them and want to show me that they are "around." For a "ghost writer" who has never actually seen a ghost, this can be exhilarating and very reassuring. It would be strange if there were no human residue, no remnants of the lives that were once lived in these old Port Byron homes. Layers of living haven't been swept away here. This Erie town's history is her greatest strength.

No Name Cemetery

In this wild and romantic countryside, where you can still walk a mile without meeting a living soul, there is a small cemetery that bears mentioning here since ghostly figures have been seen floating above the headstones, and sometimes standing in the middle of the road.

This cemetery looked harmless; a bare, lowland quadrangle forgotten for years! It is now covered with weeds and brush in which, hidden underneath tall pine trees, the few graves with their sunken headstones seem lost and lonely in the expanse of the moonlight. But at the stroke of midnight, on certain unspecified nights, there appeared an apparition which is claimed to be that of a local farmer, who died in the early 1900s.

Years ago a curious tale was told:

One damp foggy night, a young woman and her male companion stopped their fancy sportscar at this out-of-the way farmhouse to ask for help. The farmhouse, which is approached by a narrow winding lane from the main road, stands hidden in a kind of shallow basin of land; a few acres ploughed but mostly marshes. They told the farmer that they were waiting for money from her parents. Living alone in the big house for several years after his wife's death, the farmer was finally persuaded to let them stay on until their traveling money arrived.

The couple's car was seen parked in the farm's driveway for three days.

The farmer was found murdered.

Some say he was robbed and killed by these two strangers, but no one really knows what happened there.

Many of the neighbors were worried and fearful. This was the beginning of the greatest mystery ever in this area.

I made a few inquiries to our local historians, Carner and Marie, and learned that a John Jetty was murdered in 1908. The interesting thing is that we may be talking about the same farmer.

At the No Name Cemetery an inscription on one of the old headstones reads:

JETTY, JOHN   1840-1908
MARY   1841-1888

The Jetty murder is unsolved to this day.

One morning not long afterwards an unexplained figure was seen riding a black horse over the marshes. They say it was an unobtrusive piece of marsh ground that had a beauty and mystery all its own, especially at dusk when a mist often hovered there.

Ghostly whispers and half-interpreted sounds had been reported and some unexplained figures had been seen at the place many called "Murder Swamp."

Occasionally as darkness gathered about the marshes, this phantom form was seen by dozens of people. Scores more heard about it but no one had the courage to approach it.

Bizarre tales of this spirit continued to circulate in the surrounding neighborhood all through the century. Some of these stories were eerie and frightening. But despite the ghost talk and sightings, the local constable said he did not believe there was any such thing as a ghost spirit and he would not investigate any more reports of them. However, he and his assistant searched some of the places where the spirit had been seen and found absolutely nothing. But for a time, several all-night vigils were kept by the two officers.

I was told that the apparition was seen so often, some years ago, that the singular appearances ceased to attract attention and came to be accepted by the townspeople. All except Marie, Mentz's historian, who was ten years old at the time. She told me of this inexplicable happening.

Marie and the family maid, Grace, always picked thimbleberries in the marshes behind Jetty's house. One day when they were busy filling their baskets, Grace saw something moving in the shadows of the berry bushes. Then a dark patch of air formed around her. Quickly it disappeared leaving her mesmerized. She couldn't say anything to little Marie, but somehow she lifted her up and made a bungling rush for the towpath road and home.

Still not much was to be made of the momentary vision, but it was the end of their berry picking in the marshes.

It is still possible to trace people who remember the Jetty murder but are reluctant to admit having seen his ghost.

This ghost seems to have disappeared for years until recently when an employee from the nearby sugar beet plant had a frightening experience. He told me that driving home from work late one night, he saw, standing in the middle of the road, a "spirited form." He couldn't stop his truck in time and drove through the translucent body. After a horrified moment, he saw the spirit speed, magically swift, to the far side of the road and into the open field.

Did the ghostly figure come from the ancient cemetery? Some of the old timers believe that it was John searching for his murderers.

For that reason, over the years, the road that leads past this No Name Cemetery was avoided—especially during the full moon season.

Believe me, even in the daylight, this road is spooky but on a dark night it can give you the creeps.

The White Bustle

Aunt Rose and her boyfriend were talking near the garden fence, when suddenly her bustle fell to her knees. Horrified, she quickly asked her boyfriend to look at the beautiful heavens filled with sparkling stars. As he gazed upwards, she quickly scooped up her bustle and hurled it over the fence.

The boy saw the white object flying through the air and left screaming, "A ghost! It's a ghost!" and left Aunt Rose to walk back home alone. Before she reached her house, the neighborhood men were racing past her, guns loaded, ready to charge the ghost.

Auntie, having retrieved her bustle, was smiling to herself.

Witch's Spell

An uncommonly ugly old woman thrust her way into the small grocery store on Main Street followed by several women, men and children.

Frightened, Mrs. Saverese, owner of the small business, immediately drew the curtains across the closet hiding her grandson, Tony, and Jumpty who was there to buy bread for her mom. She told the children not to say one word.

The gypsies took everything in sight but the homemade bread which Mrs. Saverese refused to give them. In the days that followed, mysterious bad luck came to the little store. Bread rose to the ceiling or fell flat as a pancake; the fresh fruits and vegetables became moldy overnight and pandemonium broke out in the store after she went to bed.

Three times the ugly old woman appeared and went back to the store to demand the bread.

On her last visit, Mrs. Saverese wondered if supernatural powers were not at work and gave her the bread.

"The spell is broken," cackled the old gypsy witch, and she disappeared.

Visitation at Death

By visitation at death, I mean that the spirit of a person at the exact instant of death seems to cause itself to be seen by some friend or relative. This phenomenon is known around the world. It can assume forms other than that of the dying person such as in the form of a bright light.

"In truth," he began, "I have never seen the ghosts that so many people talk about. I have, however, had a number of experiences at about the time of the death of an acquaintance or relative of mine.

"The first happened about 1910, in the days when you didn't put on a new wheel when you had a flat tire. I had just finished fixing a flat, when I heard a sound like an immense rock hitting the road, but there was nothing there. Suddenly, a bright light circled my car and shot up towards the stars. I don't mind admitting I was scared stiff and drove off as fast as I could!

"When I arrived home, my wife told me that my best friend had just died. It was about the same time that I had seen the bright light.

"I have not only heard of the fireball light seen on tombstones, or under the eaves of homes, but even just standing in mid-air and always disappearing into the sky.

"Many people have reported seeing at the cemetery, a flicker of white light that floated from tree to tree in the shadowy moonlit nights. It harmed no one. Another lost soul, I figure."

From a nurse of my acquaintance, I quote verbatim:

"I know no one dies alone; there is always someone to welcome him and guide him to his new home. While watching over the bed of a dying patient, I would discern spirit forms around the bed whom I took to be dead relatives, and as life retreated from the body of the patient, a pearly white mist would begin to gather over the body until is assumed the shape of the person.

"Then the person, shining with an ethereal light slowly joined the ghostly forms around him and all disappeared into the misty air."

Ruth's Intercom Cries

Nine o'clock . . . p.m.

Ruth called me and mentioned she had written a long letter to me but hadn't had the time to finish it and mail it off . . . but she thought I would enjoy the story about her grandchild and . . . perhaps their house is haunted. . . .

Well, of course I immediately picked up my pad and pen and got ready for her story. Ruth doesn't think it is too spooky, trying very hard to be intelligent about it all . . . but it seems that her granddaughter was in the guest room in her portable crib . . . they have a monitor in the room for the baby and another monitor in

5

Ruth's bedroom so she can keep a close watch on her.

Through the monitor speaker came the baby's crying voice and Heather, the baby's mother, ran upstairs to bring little Blakie downstairs. The family was talking and enjoying a snack when they heard a baby's cry coming from the monitor. Both Ruth and Heather looked over at the baby who was not crying, but was smiling at them. Again, a crying baby's voice came over the speaker. Ruth ran upstairs to check out the crying and as she entered the room, she heard the last weak cry of a baby. Looking out of the window, she could see no one. Then she checked her mom's room and she was asleep.

Back downstairs, Ruth's husband and son, Jeff, tried to find an explanation for the baby's crying voice coming from the monitor speaker. Every time Ruth joined the family, the cries could be heard.

The cries lasted but a few seconds but it seemed like hours to them. Was their monitor picking up waves of another monitor or was it supernatural?

But then, as Ruth said, we have no neighbors with babies!

Phone Calls

Kathy told me of a friend on Owasco Lake Road who had a favorite granddaughter, and after her friend's death, her granddaughter had some rather frightening days.

Every evening her dead grandmother phones her. The calls continue to this very day!

Haunted Abbey

To the south of Auburn stands the old abbey with its spectral monks, phantom voices and ghost bells.

The abbey stood desolate for many years, a silent sentinel with

its ghosts.

There is a holy-water stoop in a niche there, where stories have it that ghostly monks have been seen, sometimes a whole procession, slowly winding its silent way amongst the worn-looking rooms.

Sounds of soft music have been heard with voices chanting Latin and bells sweetly chiming. Some visitors remark they often smelled the burning of incense.

As soon as I heard about this haunted abbey from Jungle, I spent the next several days investigating these stories of the strange experiences he vouched for.

I found Jungle to be an astute and kindly young man, level-headed and sensible with an infectious sense of humor. He has a gift for looking on the bright side of things. He never had experienced any allegedly paranormal phenomena until his friend, Diamond, asked him to move into the then-vacant abbey with him to help keep the place clean and free of vandals. Diamond's brother was about to turn the abbey into apartments.

The two men, now occupying the monastery, decided to wear some of the old monks' clothing to a Halloween party. They even loaned the robes to some of their closest friends for the occasion. Little did they know what was to follow that evenings' partying.

The first strange happenings for which they could find no explanation were typical poltergeist activities, door rattlings and knocking. Jungle said, "Yes, it wasn't long before things happened that suggested to us that there was something haunting about the place." He and several of his buddies decided to spend the winter in the downstairs rooms to save heat and money and besides, the upstairs was too scary and noisy.

Almost immediately the abbey was reported to be plagued by movement of objects without human contact, and unexplained appearances of phantom lights. Furniture was moved upstairs and downstairs at night time; stone and grass were continually flying about the rooms and the men were kept busy sweeping and cleaning up and replacing articles in their correct places.

Jungle complained that the doors would lock without anyone being at home, then unlock without any difficulty. There were incidents when food and clothing were moved and unaccountably appeared or disappeared.

Late one evening, they heard noises from the direction of the bathroom. The noises were described as rappings and scratchings that sometimes lasted all through the night. Not unnaturally, these sounds were at first blamed on mice and squirrels who had taken over the place. Things became so bad that no lamp or candle would remain lit—even a candle especially blessed and sprinkled with holy water. Upon investigation nothing was ever visible and no explanation or cause for the noise was ever found.

The rappings continued with regularity for several weeks. Unexplained odors joined the wealth of phenomena at the abbey. Once a strong smell of lilacs permeated the whole building. These flowers were completely out of season— it was January! And the smell of baking bread came often late at night. There had once been a large oven built into the brick wall in the kitchen.

Jungle said the cupboard doors were found open every morning. He told me that he had no doubt whatever that the abbey was haunted by at least one robed figure which he thought was probably a former monk who died there. Once he found himself within a few feet of this ghostly figure on a Sunday morning when Diamond had gone to church and had locked the door behind him. Jungle was cleaning off the breakfast dishes and putting things away in the cupboard when he saw the fully robed monk immediately in front of him. He was about to ask him how he got in when it bent down and seemed to be searching for something. The ghostly monk straightened up and faded away into the brick wall.

He didn't know then that a week later he would hear the voice of a young person singing in the rectory. It resembled a plain singing chant. As the singing stopped, it was followed by the sounds of footsteps lightly walking past him and up the stairway. Nothing was visible but the footsteps continued across the rooms until early morning.

Recently Jungle said that there have been more sightings of ghostly figures at the abbey. One person reported the apparition of a white-robed mysterious person who glided across the lawn from the main building toward the garden and simply vanished, seemingly into thin air. Another tenant claimed that a dark-cloaked figure, misty and shadowy, crossed the doorway as he was about to enter.

One of the carpenters working for the present owner, asked who the priest was who watched him so intently and who seemed to be there one minute and gone the next. Another worker ran up from the sunken swimming pool in the dungeon-like cellar, looking very frightened, and said he had passed a robed figure on the stairs who had disappeared into one of the old walls.

As befits such an historical building, Diamond and Jungle believe the old abbey has a ghost, a monk dressed in a brown robe who is forever bound to the grounds. It is rumored that this spirit of a monk has been seen gliding slowly along the garden path and disappears behind the carriage house across the street. The hood of the clothing which the monk wore, covered his face so that no features were discernible. Irene, a tenant, has seen the apparition but once, but it was so frightening, she refused to cross the street alone after dark.

On their last night in the old abbey, Jungle and Diamond heard something they had never been able to explain. It was a curious, loud, rolling sound, like a huge bowling ball being rolled over the wooden floors upstairs. After a few seconds it stopped; then it began again and it was heard intermittently throughout the night. Never before and never afterwards. Perhaps I should check with the owner before accepting such a statement.

These young men are still puzzled by the things that happened to them during their brief stay at the abbey. When asked if they would ever consider moving back there, both remarked, "Yes, of course. Where else can you live with a holy ghost?"

Trizzy

Every town has its story tellers and Port Byron has a rich Irish and Italian oral tradition. The body of myths and history, folk and fairy tales; the knowledge of herbs, of medicine, ways of caring for the sick or predicting the weather; the poems and songs of prayers and superstitions. All this was passed on from one generation to the next.

By 1940, Trizzy was old and I needed to remember these old tales. She would sit in her favorite overstuffed sofa chair and tell me about our town back in the early Erie Canal days. She lived with my great-grandmother, Marguerite, for many years after her arrival from the old country. She said she could still see her standing by the open fire and holding a hot coal above her stone pipe, trying to light it, while watching them out of the corner of her eye.

I usually sat in silence, studying their facial expressions as Trizzy and neighbors talked around me. When Trizzy did tell her stories, she cautioned us to avoid the company of the "evil eye" doers. She knew them all—most of the time they were her neighbors or some acquaintance from another town.

Trizzy had some peasant superstitions which few people could equal for wildness and incredibility. My grandmother did not take them too seriously but they amused the family. Her friends said that Trizzy's fireside tales were of the most ghostly kind.

A few were exceedingly picturesque. There was, for instance, the belief that had nothing to do with ghosts. It was most earnestly believed and frequently practiced and, I might add, with apparent success. If your fruit tree has reached an age where you thought it should have started to bear but had not, it could be made fruitful by getting up before sunrise on Good Friday and hitting it with a stick three times! It worked for Trizzy and her small fruit orchard.

She also warned that one should *never* rock an empty rocking chair. It brings bad luck. Well, her husband Charlie didn't believe any of her stories and kept rocking the chair with his heavy boots. Trizzy yelled out "Get your foot off that rocker." He had no sooner heard the order when he was struck a tremendous blow on his mouth. Kindly old Trizzy was across the room from him and only raised her hands in an "I told you so" fashion.

Trizzy possessed a large, thick, cloth-bound book containing her own herbal remedies, and this was constantly in use. The book contained many typical old Italian remedies for simple ail-

10

ments. I have always had my suspicions that she knew more about aches and pains and such than our local doctor.

Grandmother said that Trizzy had magic lore and knowledge that had been preserved from generation to generation by good and careful family members known as "healers." She was skilled by reason of birth—the powers seemed to run in families. She was trained in the use of herbs, oil and water potions, and in midwifery, as well as in the finding of lost animals, and sometimes in fortune telling.

She could also sense when "bad" visitors in her neighborhood were at work and could defeat it with her "mal-ooche" mixture of olive oil dropped into a bowl of water. The spots of oil would gather or separate as the story of evil unfolded in the water. Oil drops gathered together meant a group of bad people causing all the harm; if one drop of oil separated into two drops, double trouble was ahead. Then Trizzy would end the ritual by dipping her fingers into the oil and water bowl, run it across the clients forehead and repeat her magical prayers. Believe it or not, she cured many headaches with this treatment and chased away the evil doers at the same time.

Healing required an understanding of the use of herbs. She would prescribe lemon balm for weak stomachs, periwinkle for treatment of the skin, lavender for cough, betony as an aid against insomnia and preventative of nightmares, and a shot of whiskey for a toothache (only after the gum and tooth felt numb, were you allowed to swallow the whiskey).

With each ritual went an old-age charm. Thus the power of oil and water curing a headache was made effective by a prayer recited several times that began with "Saint Peter, or Matthew, Mark, Luke and John, bless me and this person standing before you," and ended with "whoever keeps these words for my sake shall never again have the headache" (or whatever she was curing at the time).

Trizzy told legends about saints, frivolous anecdotes and mythical enchantments, and local legends about the building of the Erie Canal and the many famous people who stopped by for food and shelter at the Saroney Boarding House. Famous names like

Joseph Jefferson and Junius Booth, who played the boards in New York, as well as other thespians who traveled the Erie Canal. She could listen to their tales once and thereafter repeat them word for word.

Even better known are her stories about supernatural beings. In each of her rooms there were small bottles of holy water on the dressers and tables and large gold framed pictures hung from her bedroom walls.

I didn't think too much of it at the time, but now I realize there is some truth to the belief that her house was haunted, as she told us. She would never stay there alone. If Charlie was at work, she visited with her neighbors until he returned. She had many haunting incidents and believed there was a body buried in her cellar. Most people said she was making it all up or was too superstitious; that sort of fit the pattern as to why the holy water was around.

She also had the ability to recognize a witch. There are not usually many outward signs except the so-called witch-marks on trees, brooms twitching and moving as one entered a room and eerie eye movements. Trizzy could recognize a witch from a distance and would immediately sprinkle herself and friends with holy water which she frequently carried in her apron pocket.

Many of her neighbors were aware of her powers. They came to her with their problems and sought guidance in their lives.

At one time people believed in "scrying," a method of obtaining psychic information on the past, present or future through images on a reflecting surface, such as a crystal ball or water. Trizzy used to scry using a large soup bowl filled with cold water. Her clients, mostly relatives and neighbors, projected personal influences into this by slowly bending heads over the bowl while Trizzy dropped olive oil from her finger tips into the water. Trizzy was an excellent scryer. Curing headaches was another of her specialties. As always in her rituals, she rubbed the oil-water mixture on the client's forehead, while repeating those special prayers. Incredulously, perhaps, images sometimes appeared in the bowl.

Trizzy was an old woman now and we refused to believe that

she was approaching senility. We rationalized that a lot of ninety-year-old women walked the roads searching for their dead husbands, talking to themselves. But most of the relatives insisted that Trizzy was "losing it." Normal old people didn't give away their clothing, household things and food until there was nothing left in the house.

In time she turned quarrelsome, irritable and downright hostile toward children. She never had any of her own and couldn't relate to them even when she was much younger. But we all loved her and remember to this very day one of her witty sayings:

> If you are not handsome at twenty,
> Not strong at thirty,
> Not rich at forty,
> Not wise at fifty,
> You never will be!

Water Spirits

Fishing turns men into philosophers. Willie was a terrific fisherman. Since his time was free of all forms of gainful employment, he was able to devote himself to forecasting the weather, searching for new fishing holes and shopping around for the latest bassboats. Say nothing of the time he spent making his own colorful "buck-tail" jigs. He had in his employ, besides friends and family who worked without pay, the State Police who collected deer-tails from the dead animals found along the Thruway. It's a known fact, says Willie, that deer-tail hairs make the finest lures for bass fishing.

Willie also was always stretching and varnishing a few truths about his adventures in the great outdoors. That may be why his whole family has never been in sync about anything he does, particularly in regard to his hunting and fishing.

Though this legend sounds utterly astounding, there may be a grain of truth in it.

Now Marr was another fisherman who could be described as

one of the "good olde country boys," with a thick John Wayne accent. He and Willie spent many late hours discussing and planning their fishing expeditions, and their fish stories, always entertaining, helped keep this friendship going for over forty years. However, the latest Marr incident hasn't convinced Willie that his buddy has all his oars in the water.

As Marr tells it:

"I was down there fishing when I saw one. Oh, I can spend all day telling about that water-spirit, but very few of my friends will believe me, because the spirits don't appear with any degree of regularity. They can show up at any time of the day or night, and then never 'gain for months. Fishermen around here refuse to talk about anything that spooky, not even Willie, who swears he had never seen one, but for some reason is afraid to go fishing alone! I don't give a hoot, I tell it the way I see it and that's all."

Marr had a gratifying array of anecdotes, but this next one is my favorite.

It was the first day of trout season and Willie and Marr took out crumpled-up dollar bills for their "biggest fish" bets. It seems that this has been going on ever since their high-school days. The money is put into an empty coffee can and stored underneath the cab seat. In the past it has helped them buy gas, cigarettes, beer, worms and occasionally the latest issue of "Fish-finder" magazine.

The fishing in Salt Creek was as fine as any they had ever seen; they wouldn't have any trouble catching their limits today. They dumped out the worm cans and started fishing. After they had a good string of fish and started for shore, they suddenly realized that their boat was swinging too far to the right. Suddenly, a gust of wind whipped Marr's line around Willie and buried the hook in the flab of his right leg. Always one for taking a bad situation and making it worse, Marr had the frightening thought that the water-spirits caused him to snag his partner.

"Crazy nonsense," Willie yelled at him. At this point he was making an effort not to hit Marr, say nothing of believing in those spirits.

The boat came to a stretch where huge willow branches reared

14

up on both sides of the stream, and the eerie late afternoon light shone on the water revealing patches of mist which drifted about like stray ghosts on a haunt.

Marr stood there quivering with fright. "You never know how to treat these spirits," he moaned.

Willie, suffering from pain, had a happy meanness to him. "This place is too quiet; a perfect spot for your evil water-spirits to hang out, indeed," he said smiling with satisfaction.

Suddenly the boat headed for a large willow tree, which hung out over the stream, raking the current with its crooked branches. They tried to steer the boat towards the shore but it failed to respond to the oars. Magically, the instant the oars touched the water something seized one of them. With a grip of steel, it drew it inexorably down into the deep, dark, airless world where "water-spirits" supposedly live. Marr was dead sure of that.

The two fishermen hesitated a moment then looked at the stream in disbelief as the water foamed around the boat. What was happening? They were calm and cool fishermen when they entered the stream earlier in the day; now, as they were making their way back from the deeper waters, this fishing trip became a nightmare.

Some force, water-spirits perhaps, was drawing them into the weeping willow, which seemed to be reaching out for them with its snarled limbs drawing them into its deadly embrace. As they drifted into a creepy section of the stream, the frightened men saw strange movements in the shape of a "V" wave. Without any warning, something ghastly grabbed Marr from behind and with enormous power jerked him out of the boat and slammed him flat on his back against the surface of the water. He was afraid the water-spirits were going to drown him. (I should mention here that Willie has offered no explanation as to what he was doing when the water-spirit pushed Marr into the water.)

Marr whined over the loss of his gear as Willie pulled him back into the boat, but it didn't take him long to realize that they were in deep trouble. They fell silent, and in the stillness the two men heard the groan of straining wood; their boat was vibrating dangerously. The cattails trembled and foamy water rippled and splashed against the boat. Suddenly from among the cattails rose a water-spirit! Infinitely mysterious and shapeless in appearance, it squealed, wafted around their heads and then dove into the murky, swirling water and disappeared. Immediately the water calmed down and the boat stopped shaking. The two men, exhausted and scared, scrambled into the creek, grabbed the boat, dragged it up the bank and shoved it onto the bed of Willie's rusty pickup truck. With a last nervous glance at the haunted fishing hole, they sped back to town. All the way Marr had the feeling a few of the more persistent water-spirits were still clinging to the boat. So he loaded up his double-barrel shotgun and aimed it out the rear window of the cab.

At the Kincaid Tavern, Willie told his buddies, "It's the queerest thing ever I've tumbled across since I've been fishing." Marr agreed with him, repeating, "I told you so, Willie, I told you so."

To this very day, Willie continues to sift the shadows of the woods around the streams for signs of "V" shaped waves!

Marr has now relocated to the next dimension. Local fishermen believe he is now a "water-spirit" looking for Willie who, by the way, ended up with all that coffee-can money and a new bassboat!

Vault Talks

Tips on haunted places come in a variety of ways, but this was a new one.

I had been having a hard time getting a good cemetery story. Lead after lead soured, an obvious phony or an unlikely, unbelievable legend or some other sort of wrong number. Suddenly a good story came by at Rooker's Veggie Stand on State Street Road.

It was Mary, owner of the small stand, who first told me of this remarkable haunting at the local cemetery vault. Her grandfather, by marriage, is the one who experienced the happenings.

The ghost may have had its origin in the mysterious death of the man buried in the vault. No one is alive now to give us his name and how he died, but one thing for sure is that he certainly scared the townspeople for many years.

Grandfather had several grandchildren who loved to play in the cemetery. One day they came home screaming that someone inside the old vault had spoken to them, and when they turned to run, there was an old woman dressed in black standing next to them. She told the children it was her late husband inside the vault. They immediately rushed home, frightened out of their wits, and wouldn't go near the place again.

According to local residents, the old woman had been conversing with her dead husband for many years. She would stand near the heavy steel-gated door and start a conversation with him; a voice from within would answer her. Talking with her husband through the vault was like having a chat in her living room and she never missed a chance to visit with him.

Grandfather didn't believe a word of it and one day decided to check this out. Besides, he didn't want the children afraid of such things as ghosts and vault voices, especially in their favorite playground.

Late one afternoon, he hid behind the vault and watched the woman approach and stand near the gate; she slowly walked up to the steel door of the vault and called her husband's name, "Hennesy." Suddenly a voice from within answered, "Yes," and she then started to tell him of her daily problems and talk about life in general. The ghostly voice within the vault would answer usually with one word or at the most two.

Grandfather said that he stood by the old vault terror-stricken because the voice was indeed coming from within the concrete vault.

He said the children ran ahead of him so fast that he soon was left alone in the cemetery with the old woman. She never said a word to him but continued to talk with whoever was inside the vault drawer!

The cemetery and the vault both remain to this day. Should you happen to make a visit to the graves, make a side trip to the moss-covered vault and knock on the iron-gate door. If a ghostly voice calls out from within, ask him his wife's whereabouts. I need it for this story's ending!

Phantom of the Theater

Around the turn of the century, a famous theater boasted of vaudeville acts and performers who would make their mark on Hollywood's early years. W.C. Fields and Fanny Brice were just two of the greats who performed there. Now the old theater has picked up a ghost to entertain as well.

Actors, stagehands and night watchmen at the theater began to tell eerie stories of a ghost wandering the backstage area. Paul, who works on the plays, has had some frightening experiences there as well.

At first he didn't believe these scary tales but when he saw the phantom actor appear on the stairway and then fade away into nothingness, he became a strong believer.

One of the jobs Paul had was to turn out the lights after a performance, but being afraid to enter the rooms, he would reach into them and turn off the light switch from the hallway. One night as he was walking along the hallway, he heard the all too familiar footsteps of the phantom and ran to tell his co-workers, but they had heard them too.

One old man working there was found dead in the dressing room and they all teased, but with some seriousness, that he probably heard those ghostly steps and died of a heart attack. They were that frightening.

The ghost was blamed for many strange phenomena at the theater. Once, the producer and stagehand were talking in a room when an ashtray flew into the air, only inches away from them. Ropes holding stage backdrops often vibrated and swayed by themselves and stagehands swore that the ropes would stop moving only when they were ordered to!

One group of actors said the ghost was once an actor who became deeply depressed and hung himself in the basement of the

18

building and now returns to haunt the theater. Paul thinks that could be possible; he lived in a haunted house. It was a lovely home but very spooky. His playroom was haunted and he had trouble keeping the toys off the ceiling! The former owner hanged himself in that room. Paul is not saying where the house is located but it is somewhere in Port Byron!

Paul said that recently there were untraceable odors detected all over the stage and a ghostly voice called out the leading lady's name during a night performance. The play continued but it scared everyone into traveling in twos for the rest of the theater season.

Sometimes the ghost is seen standing in the back where it disappears into the ceiling. The theater ghost is regarded as foretelling a successful production at the theater, but as Paul says, "When seen or heard in the hallways, it becomes an unfriendly phantom!"

Goodbye Sammy

On the 18th of October, Jackie was lying on her bed suffering from a bad cold, and grieving over the death of her brother, Sammy, who died unexpectedly from a gunshot wound earlier that week.

Suddenly she heard the sound of the front door opening, followed by heavy footsteps climbing the stairs towards her bedroom. The footsteps ceased and she heard the sounds of movement within her room.

Nothing visible, but she knew she was not alone. She felt the foot of her bed sag, the mattress was definitely pushed down from a weight on it. She was startled but not afraid.

Jackie saw a figure seated at the foot of the bed. She stared at it for several seconds, her head spinning, her heart pounding. She blinked and looked again. She couldn't believe her eyes. The figure was Sammy!

Then she heard, in deep and hollow tones as if calling from the mysterious confines of the spirit-land, his voice that was not a voice, that spoke, yet did not speak. It was as a whisper which she both sensed and heard, saying, "I'm all right, Jackie, don't worry."

She could not speak but mentally she was communicating with him. There was an indescribable sadness about his presence and his voice.

Without another word, Sammy's figure arose, turned and left the room.

"Goodbye Sammy," Jackie called out lovingly.

She heard again the heavy footsteps echo through the stairway as he slowly made his way downstairs, and the door open and shut as he left her home for the last time.

Gambler's Ghost

This former hotel is reputed to be haunted by a tall gambler in a black coat, who seems to be searching for someone or something.

In the early 1800s, the barroom had round oak tables and chairs. It is believed there is still one of the original gambling tables in the old building.

Back in the hotel's heydays, the place sported roulette wheels, shuffling cards and rolling dice. All illegal but well hidden from the proper authorities.

The history of this place is most intriguing.

One story is told of a stranger walking into the barroom around midnight and ordering a shot of whiskey. There were only three customers in the place, a very slow evening. The bartender set a glass in front of the man and then started closing up. When he came back from the wine cellar, one of the customers, a guy who looked like Abe Lincoln, said, "You know this place is haunted." He said he had seen something that walked behind the bar and knocked over a whiskey bottle. The other customers laughed and teased, "It's the ghost of Johnnie Walker," but then became aware that the stranger was missing, his whiskey glass was empty and no one had seen him leave the place. On inspection they found no one in the rooms, but still could hear footsteps moving about upstairs.

One waitress said someone would order a drink and it would be gone before they had a chance to drink it. People would find their cigars smashed—sometimes stolen. Apparently the ghost didn't like cigars.

The former owner's explanation of the hauntings is that during a game of cards a saloon customer was caught cheating and was shot on the spot. The wounded gambler staggered to the bar where he later died.

The fatal game of cards is supposed to have taken place during the late hours of the night and it is during these hours that the disturbances at the old hotel reach their climax.

Next time you stop for a beer and a mustached, black-suited gambler bellies up to the bar and orders a drink, only to disappear when served, don't panic. It's the ghost!

The Best Bon Bons

The most dramatic event of Samuel's life happened in 1905 when he was living in Wheaton with his cousin Patsy and Patsy's wife, Pauline.

Pauline and Patsy had been married for over ten years and were childless. There was nothing he wouldn't do for his wife's happiness, but Pauline wanted a child. Finally, she took a job at the nearby chocolate factory, at the advice of her family doctor. It didn't take her very long to start enjoying life with parties and outings with her fellow workers. Patsy was glad to see his young wife smiling and laughing again.

Then Patsy died suddenly of a heart attack, or so the friendly doctor wrote on the death certificate. But the family knew better . . . Patsy died of food poisoning . . . chocolate poisoning to be exact, made with the aid of the doctor.

Pauline had continued her therapy with the doctor and the two soon became lovers. "They were happy beyond the power of words," as the family gossip, Patsy's sister Nellie, announced at Patsy's funeral.

Pauline did admit to the authorities that she had given Patsy special chocolate candy that night but that he had requested it. She made the best candy in the shop, she boasted. The case was dropped when the doctor gave testimony that Patsy was not well, lived a fast life and was warned to slow down earlier that year.

A respectable time went by and the doctor and Pauline were married. Samuel moved out after the candy episode. He remembered that Pauline had offered him a chocolate bon-bon but when he reached for it, something pushed his hand away. It happened a second time and he decided to forget it. To this very day, his children and grandchildren believe it was his dead mother's spirit that knocked the candy from his hand and saved his life.

Pauline and her sweetheart doctor lived in the "Nob Hill" section of town and were accepted in "high society," as Pauline called it. It was a dream come true.

But her happiness didn't last long. She went blind soon after their last European vacation. Relatives said it was the doctor again, others said it was God's punishment for her treatment to Patsy. Whatever, Pauline never again enjoyed her new life as a doctor's wife. Gone were her elegant parties and expensive vacation. She was confined to her home with her five cats and several dogs.

Pauline, totally blind could no longer see her beloved doctor but *she could see Patsy.*

His ghost haunted her until the day she died.

Fay's Happy Birthday!

All seemed quiet on the "supernatural" front for many years in the southwest section of this small Erie town. Only recently have the spirits made their appearance throughout the county and particularly on Burnt Hill.

The Dubois home was where Fay was born many years ago. It has been in her family for over one hundred years. But when she died, family members didn't know what to do about this very large estate. They moved in and immediately started remodeling the place, and things suddenly began happening that could not be explained in a rational way. But it didn't scare Kathy. This was her childhood dream—fixing up the old homestead.

One evening after a long day of painting, papering and general repairs in the downstairs, she decided to take an early bath and retire to her newly decorated bedroom. It was beautiful with the new carpeting and curtains . . . the new bedspread matched the curtains; she had designed and sewn them in one evening, she bragged to her friends.

When she turned off the light near her bedstand, she saw a vision of her mom standing in the doorway. Her mom had died twenty years ago that month. She stared at her, speechless, so scared that she had to close her eyes.

Then she heard her mom call out her name . . . "Kathy, Kathy."

Quickly she opened her eyes again and found her mom now standing in the middle of the room. Kathy was now so frightened that she reached over and turned on the light. The apparition was gone. Kathy was not asleep; she was awake all during the happening and she is certain it was not just a dream.

The next morning, Kathy found her mom's birth certificate, old and crumpled up from years in the cellar. It stated that Fay was born in the family home at precisely the same time, same day, and same month that Kathy had seen the vision—only seventy years earlier!

Ghost Dog

It doesn't take a dramatic encounter with a ghost to be aware of them. The presence can be felt in a room with a change in an air current or by a sixth sense.

Along lonely country roads, in graveyards, and down dark, spooky lanes spirits are on the move in this world. But sometimes it is hard to say what's really happening. One thing I know is that they often scare us and we seem to enjoy things from the unknown, especially late at night.

"There's not much to this story, really," Liza said. "All I know is that after one of the Baptist Church meetings for sinners, my neighbor and I were walking home and my friend said, 'Don't walk there. Can't you see that ghost?' "

"When I looked down at the sidewalk, I did see the ghostly shape of an animal near me. At first I thought it was a real dog. Within a second or so it was very obvious that it was a fairly large dog. It just seemed to walk on air, that ghostly black dog. It scared the heck out of me and my friend. And I'll never be able to explain it to myself or my family. That is, rationally.

"It was very, very strange and I'll never forget it!"

That Bloody Stain

Elaine and her husband Gary were seated at the Legion bar making some interesting ghost story talk. After awhile Gary said, rather sheepishly, that he once worked on a house that was haunted. Of course I immediately started mentally recording his words. He was working on a house on Holly Street in Auburn—a roofing job, when the owner said his house was haunted. Gary sort of laughed and asked him "how," and that's when he invited Gary inside to show him.

The owner lifted an area rug and showed Gary a red spot on the living room floor—blood, he explained. "This floor has been sanded and refinished many times by the former owner and now me, but we cannot remove that blood spot for very long. The longest the spot has remained unseen is two weeks, then after a night of bizarre happenings, the red blood spot reappeared as if it had just happened. Story has it that a man was murdered here on this spot and his blood remains—his ghost appears to be looking for revenge. It is said, he will not let them forget that horrible murder."

Gary told me that the blood spot was examined by professionals and they determined that it was blood, a spot almost the size of a human body.

It's very eerie—the red blood stain still haunts this home.

This story was told to me on Friday the 13th, 1988.

The Butterfly

Mary said that recently she had an interesting experience. She had been to her daughter's wedding on Saturday and danced with an old acquaintance. It was her first dance in years and the first since her hip operation.

Everyone there gave her a standing ovation and cried out, "Go for it Grandma . . . we love you!" She had more attention than the bride, she said, laughing shyly.

Back at home later that day, as she sat in her easy chair in front of her vegetable and fruit stand, a huge butterfly landed on her shoulder. She shooed it away but it wouldn't go; again and again, she tried to get that butterfly off her shoulder. It was the same shoulder the gentleman tapped when he asked her to dance at the wedding.

Finally after four hours of this pesky butterfly, she yelled out, "Fred, get the hell off my shoulder and leave me alone." That butterfly flew away up into the blue sky and hasn't returned. "It was my dead husband, Fred, I know. He probably was telling me that he saw me dancing!"

The Ghost Loves Music

The night was warm and a full moon shone on the old home on Main Street.

May, at age ninety or so, died. It was a sad day for the town residents, as she was special to all who knew her. A very lovely

25

maiden lady with a healthy attitude toward young people and her Catholic church. Her lovely old home and all its furnishings, including her fashionable wardrobe were sold at an auction. It didn't take long to sell her belongings; some had waited years for this day. There were crystal candlestick holders, fine linens, sterling tea sets and antiques that made the dealers practically run over one another to make their buys.

One family was lucky enough to get the house and have enjoyed remodeling it. With their two children around to play with their many toys, life became somewhat hectic at times, so the mother decided to pack some of the children's playthings and store them in the attic.

Shortly afterwards, she heard music coming from the attic and rushed upstairs to investigate. As soon as she opened the door, the music stopped. She shook her head and walked downstairs. As she descended, she was stopped in her tracks as the music box started playing once again. She walked slowly to the door again, opened it widely, but saw no one. The music had stopped. She noticed her daughter's music book opened on top of the box of other books. She closed the book and placed it back along the inside of the box, having to squeeze it gently in to get it to fit. She left the attic and went back downstairs. A few minutes later, she heard the same music sound. She rushed upstairs and again, and as soon as she opened the attic door, the music stopped. And again she found the same book opened on top of the box. She told her husband about it and he just laughed.

Not until recently did he start to believe in ghosts. This time a child's battery-operated music box started playing in the basket in the upstairs hallway. It couldn't be, the batteries were dead, they knew that for sure and had stored the toy until the day they could buy more. But to be really sure, they checked the batteries by putting them in the alarm system. Nothing. In the flashlight, nothing. So she put them back into the toy for another test.

That night around midnight, they heard music coming from the toy. Her husband got out of bed, turned on the hall light, but there was no one in the hall and the toy had stopped playing its music. He says he thinks their ghost is doing this to amuse itself, or should he say herself. May did like music; perhaps she is enjoying her home again after all.

A few months ago, the husband was home alone and heard the unmistakable sound of the music box stored in the attic. His wife often hears the sound of the musical toy being played when she stands at the bottom of the stairs.

Play It Again

She sat upright in her bed. It sounded as though a pair of giant hands had crashed down on the keys of the piano, bringing forth a terrific and hideous cacophony, a horrible jangling discord.

She rushed to the music room, turned on the light and saw that there was no one there. She tried to find a rational explanation for this astonishing happening—and at that appalling hour.

She stood there petrified, wondering what she should do next. Her hair was damp with sweat. She turned to check the door near the hallway, and then again the most dreadful sound she had ever heard in her life came from the piano. It was then that she saw the figure . . . milky and translucent. Speechless, choking with emotion, she ran from the room.

A few nights later, when her family was visiting, they heard noises again from an adjoining corridor that led to a locked cellar door. They investigated and saw nothing, but did feel a sudden icy gust of air. That was enough to call it a night!

There are many other stories of objects that mysteriously move off the piano, of doors that open and shut. Whatever it all means, one thing is certain; the ghost is still around.

The Ghostly Marine

It seems that Marine Private Sara was having a difficult time adjusting to military life. After much suffering over commands, kitchen duties and no furloughs, Sara decided to end her life. The barracks was empty and she took advantage of a small beam and hanged herself.

One night when she came home rather late from guard duty, Marine Private Kelly saw another marine standing by her bunk. She was dressed in her fatigues and had a smile on her face. Kelly looked and smiled back, but then noticed the marine was fading away. She thought it was the poor lighting at first and didn't mention it to anyone because she wasn't sure of anything—it all happened so fast.

A week later, Kelly was resting on her bunk when the same woman marine appeared. This time Kelly could see that it was not a solid body, it seemed to be floating a few feet off the floor.

Kelly screamed and the entity disappeared.

This time she told her CO and roommates. She proceeded to describe what she had seen floating near her bunk. She had tried to scream but then something unexpected happened. The entity's head left its body. "I can only tell you that I had never in all my life seen anything more terrifying than that head," Kelly explained to her friends.

The roommates all knew the ghost and had seen her many times; it was Sara coming back to visit her old barracks. She sometimes was seen near her bunk, in the hallway and sometimes floating above their heads.

"I'll tell you, anybody who doesn't believe in supernatural phenomena should have been there when ghostly Pvt. Sara came crashing into our barracks," Kelly concluded.

TV Guest

Some researchers into the paranormal believe that pieces of furniture can hold energy within them that can be released from time to time. I am not one to get bogged down in those theories because it takes away the fun of a good ghost story. This frightening story is worth telling and preserving for future TV viewers.

I listened intently, knowing I was hearing a story true and unadorned.

"It was November 1987, three days before Thanksgiving. I don't think my holidays will ever pass without remembering this strange and unbelievable incident.

"As most of my family and friends know I am a 'night' person. I watch Carson, then Letterman and even the 'Holy Rollers' after all the stations have gone off the air. This particular night, the Carson Show had just ended and the commercials were on, and I sat at the end of the sofa waiting for the next show to start. As I looked at the TV screen, I saw something out of the corner of my eye, to the left of the TV about halfway up the side, centered between the window curtain and the TV screen. It was suspended in midair and seemed to be floating but only in that one position, not moving up or down—just there! I asked myself, 'What is that?' and put on my glasses for a closer view. It looked like the skull of a small child, but it couldn't be, I kept repeating out loud. As I studied it more closely, by darn, it was a small skull suspended in the air.

"I couldn't take my eyes off the skull. I wasn't afraid because I was in shock and trying to figure it out. As I have told my family, I don't believe in ghosts and I have made that known to all who ask me.

"Well, I finally decided it was a reflection off the TV set. So I glanced quickly at it and there was nothing but a food commercial about pizza bread. I quickly looked back to the skull; it had moved to above the TV and was floating slowly along the wall above my head. Now I did get scared and closed my eyes pulling a blanket over my head at the same time.

"The Letterman Show came on and I could hear his monologue. That's when I decided to take another peek at the screen; the skull was floating off to the side again. I couldn't stand another minute of this suspense and jumped up to touch it and it vanished right before my eyes. There was nothing, absolutely nothing, near the set.

"I decided to check the outside porch light, thinking perhaps it was some unusual shadow coming in though the blinds, but the light was off—total darkness outside—no moon, not even a star. Only a few dark gray clouds skudded across the sky from time to time.

"Whatever it was, it looked very real to me and I don't believe I was asleep because I remember looking at the screen to check out the program and this skull . . . they were not together!

"The skull was rather smoky in color, not ghostly white, not a solid look to it either but rather flimsy. It was perfect in shape, eye sockets especially. I can't remember the mouth, but the eyes were very piercing and I was drawn to them more than the rest of the skull. I felt it was trying to communicate with me all along. Now I wish I had spoken to it.

"Do I believe in ghosts? I have more respect for them now.

"One more thing, it has changed my life. I am constantly checking that corner of my TV set and sadly but true, I no longer enjoy my late night programs."

Dream With a Punch

Liza told this story to her family and friends and to this very day, they all believe it was the ghost of her dead husband who paid her a visit late one full moon night.

In her dream, Liza's husband came home from work and was getting ready for his "night out with boys" at the local tavern. Liza was never invited to party with him; her job was to stay at home with their twelve children and cook, sew, clean and make sure they went to school and to church on Saturday.

He turned to Liza and asked where his white shirt was . . . he always wore it to such affairs, and she knew it, but she hadn't washed it and for a good reason. She took the dirty shirt out of the hamper and handed it to him saying, "Here it is—wear it —lipstick stains and all."

Well, he was shocked. He became furious and tore the shirt from her hands and then punched her in the stomach. The pain was so severe that Liza sat up in bed and screamed. When fully awake, she felt her stomach and the pain was still there.

The dream and stomach pain disappeared as soon as she made a trip downstairs . . . a long way from that haunted bedroom!

Haunts on the Hill

This house looked haunted from the day it was built. As far back as the early 1800s, the occupants always complained of unexplained events. Some of these incidents scared them, others were rather amusing, but the ghostly appearances made living there unbearable at the end of the forties. The house was sold several times and the last tenant who had the most problems lived there for many years after her husband's sudden death. She and her young son showed no signs of being frightened of their eerie lifestyle.

Scores of spooky incidents have been recorded.

Jim, a close neighbor, said that the old rocking chair in the haunted house would rock away with no one in it or even near it. Mrs. B, the owner, would ignore the rocking and continue her conversation with him.

The house was in complete darkness most of the time except for candles glowing here and there. Once Jim was standing in the candle-lit hallway and felt an icy breath on the back of his neck. He left the house on a fast run.

Why Mrs. B and her son spoke in whispers, Jim could never figure out. She never once yelled at him and his buddies for sneaking around the grounds late at night. Always that sweet voice and strange attitude about things in general. It was as if "they" were still in mourning after all these years; her husband's pictures were everywhere and votive candles burned day and night in front of them. Mrs. B was a very religious woman and would preach the gospel if you had time to listen.

Despite all the peculiarities of the house, Jim continued to be a good neighbor. On his last unforgettable visit, he and Mrs. B were having coffee when his coffee cup seemingly rose unaided into the air and then landed in the sink without breaking! Jim had to hold on to the table to keep from fainting, while Mrs. B held onto his arm, afraid he was about to leave before she had finished her "What is a Soul?" sermon.

As Mrs. B said, "Generally ghosts, whether haunting of their own volition or called by the living, retreated to their silent realm when the disturbance that had troubled them came to an end, or an incomplete task was finished."

Jim agreed with her as he dashed out of that gloomy, dark house of haunts forever.

Muckland Monster

When the residents of this small muckland community had nothing more than candles and kerosene lamps to keep out the night's darkness, the hours between dusk and dawn brought forth many frightening ghosts and spirits.

Such was the eerie incident of the sighting of the Muck Monster—a spirit that appeared at random, as a shapeless shadow at times, or in a hastily assumed solid body. It would huddle in the ditches along the towpath and suddenly appear if a stranger walked near its hideout.

Many well-known villagers had curious and unexplained happenings to relate about this apparition. Cats and dogs are believed to be supersensitive, so perhaps some shade of a monster does live in those now murky canal waters because animals will go way out around the canal banks and muckland ditches to get to their homes.

This monster seems to have a grudge against animals and particularly cats for they disappear nightly as they travel this area so long associated with the monster. And neighbors say, "Never have so many cats suddenly disappeared as these past few years." Is that Monster still working the mucklands at night?

So ends this story, which I ask no one to believe! But do keep an open mind; it could happen to you!

Christmas Spirit

It was 3:24 a.m. when grandmother and granddaughter were awakened by a noise under the Christmas tree; bells ringing and chug, chug sounds startled them. Grandmother called out, "Chris, is that you playing with the train set?" No answer. Her seventeen-year-old grandson was staying with her and she thought he had a sleepless night and had decided to play with the train set.

Grandmother admits she was a little afraid and had to force herself to check the ruckus in the living room.

She slowly entered the room, the train lights were on and smoke was coming out of the small stack, the wheels were turning and grinding, but the train was not moving. It went through all the motions but remained in front of the decorated Christmas tree.

The train set was battery-operated with a remote control box to start and stop it; the remote control was on the fireplace mantle and nothing was near it. The cat was outside and the yellow lab was asleep on her rug in the kitchen. How did the train start? The train switch was turned on in the coal car, but it wouldn't start the train without the remote control button being pushed. She tried to work the train with the remote control button but nothing happened. Finally the train stopped working when they turned on the living room lights!

They think it was Sam's spirit, her granddaughter's dad who died earlier that year. He loved trains when he was a boy, and would spend most of his Christmas vacation under the tree working the train set.

The Weighlock Ghost

An imposing structure, the Erie Canal Museum in the thick of the Erie Boulevard district was built during the Erie Canal days as a weigh station for the boats traveling these waterways; it has remained pretty much the same to this day.

This credible story was told to me by the museum director who feels that Mr. Buchanan's ghost walks the building nightly.

"The experiences I had always happened late in the afternoon. It was usually dark outside; late fall days make the old rooms look creepy and haunted with all the heavy, dark-stained, ornate wood panelling and woodwork. Even the tin ceilings, with their fancy designs, made the building look ominous. I never saw the ghost but I would hear little noises on a shelf and soon books or antique knick-knacks would start falling to the floor. It would frustrate me. I didn't feel afraid but I would stop whatever I was doing to try to figure it out. I always tried to blame it on a large mouse, but then no signs of that kind of problem were ever visible. Besides, in the library, the museum cat was usually asleep nearby when these things started falling.

"I felt strongly that there was a presence, but I never believed that it would hurt me."

Another annoying ghostly incident was the sound resembling a heavy man pacing the floors. One night an employee was frightened nearly out of his wits and never recovered sufficiently to relate what he had seen or heard. He has since left his job as night watchman.

Witnesses abound and are quite believable. In fact, one of the witnesses was a "man of the cloth" who doesn't like to talk about this sort of thing. Some saw the classic vaporous, ghostlike image; all swore that they had seen the figure in good moonlight inside the library. All seem to agree the ghost was that of Buchanan, who once owned a fleet of canalboats during the heydays of the canal. One report described the appearance of the ghost every night during the month of October. One man made a dash at the figure but even his crowbar had no effect and the mysterious form hovered about the room until shortly after midnight. People were so terrified towards the end of that evening that they hid in the weigh station office behind the large oak desk until the form disappeared.

It was discovered that many years earlier a man had been murdered near the spot where the ghost first appeared . . . the canal weighing scales.

34

Frances' Spirit

Anna had an unusual experience which has her curiosity aroused.

It was Friday morning around ten o'clock when she first noticed a file folder on the empty desk near her. No one seemed to be working on it and after awhile she looked at it and noticed it was her brother Harry's file. She did not open it but wondered why he had business at the bank now, months after the closing date on his new home. Finally, she began asking the other workers in the mortgage department about this file and no one knew why or how the folder got on the desk or who was working on it.

Anna had had a rather sad day. It was the anniversary of her mother's death. Harry's wife, Shirley, was in the hospital, and Anna had refused to go see her; She could not take another visit there—too many bad memories of her mom's sudden death.

At closing time at the bank, the folder was still on the empty desk—Harry and Shirley's file.

Then it dawned on Anna, "It must be Mom telling me to get up to that hospital to see my very ill sister-in-law. Mom was like that—always sending her children to visit sick relatives."

At the hospital she told Shirley the story. They embraced one another and cried tears of sadness and joy.

To declare that they were not nervous on that peculiar day would be an exaggeration both gross and ridiculous. They were not in any sense childishly superstitious, but because neither Shirley nor Harry had requested their file be taken out of the bank vault, they believed in this case an overwhelming preponderance of evidence pointed to the existence of certain forces of great power—the spirit of Frances.

Barn Story

"If you go back a century or two in search of folklore, you can find in books innumerable accounts of ghosts and spirits,"

35

reporter Colley said as he prepared his papers for my interview. "That certainly was my experience. No matter what you believe, ghosts do exist!"

Then he asked, "Do you believe in them?" My answer, as always, was, "I don't know what I believe today, but I'm not afraid of ghosts."

He told me that for many years he was a confirmed skeptic but because his best friend had a frightening experience recently, he now knows there is something strange going on around us that cannot be explained logically.

As his story goes, Colley's friend had returned to the barn to take care of the cows. It was milking time and he was alone today, the other family members were busy getting the hay cut before the rain hit. The latest weather forecast called for heavy thunderstorms later that day.

As he sat on the milking stool, some unknown attraction was pulling his eyes in a seemingly irrelevant direction, and he could not help staring at a certain spot on the barn door. This farm once belonged to his beloved grandfather and he missed him very much. Then he saw his grandfather standing in the doorway. Only a few seconds passed and the ghostly figure vanished. Overcome with grief, he had to stop his work and visit his grandfather's grave immediately. Colley believes the grandfather is another spirit held to earth by a long-forgotten tragedy.

Colley's friend had another unusual experience. The German and Hungarian side of his friend's family keeps these ghost stores alive and very real. The latest eerie incident happened to his neighbor. He heard him screaming for help and arrived to find the axle of a John Deere farm tractor resting on the farmer's chest. He struggled and with all his two hundred pounds managed to get the tractor off the man. The dying neighbor whispered to him, "Take care of my wife and children, financial matters and keep the farm for my boys."

Then a voice at the end of the road called to the farmer and he got up and walked toward the misty figure waiting for him. Yet his solid, dead body was still on the ground near the tractor!

The Haunted Apartment

The setting is a restaurant in Auburn, whose owners prefer the author not to pinpoint. Their waitress, June, had mentioned that she believes in ghosts, in fact she lived with one. It all started when she and her husband rented an apartment that had a ghost living in the basement. June was a little nervous as she began her story but gazing at the ceiling, she said, "I felt the very strong presence of a male, probably elderly, in this apartment from day one."

All the noises and strange happenings occurred in the basement. The first incident was late at night after June and her husband had an argument and he decided to sleep on the sofa in the basement until June cooled down. About an hour later, he was awakened by a swift kick under the sofa cushion and a push. After being so rudely awakened, he climbed the stairs and shook his wife, demanding to know why she had kicked the sofa. Of course she knew nothing about it and suddenly realized that those ghost rumors must be true. Stories throughout the building about this ghost had made a fun evening until now. It was believed that whenever a married couple had a family spat, the ghost would interfere somehow and keep them awake most of the night with his spooky tricks.

As the story goes, years ago when the ghost and his two sisters lived in this building, he was always playing tricks on them. One of the sisters lived in the apartment June was renting. The other sister had the apartment on the opposite end of the building. Today the new tenants complain of many strange goings-on there in these same two apartments.

One of the most annoying tricks this ghost did was shut the lights off at all hours of the day and night. One evening after supper, June and her husband sat at the table sipping their coffee when they heard the switch box click off—1, 2, 3, 4, 5 clicks—lights went off all over the building, but click number 6, the basement lights, never happened. No one checked it out either; they stayed with the neighbors that night.

When June moved out of this haunted apartment, she said nothing to the new tenants because it was a subject one doesn't mention without people looking at you and wondering if you are nuts. But she did know them and, meeting them in the mall one day, she decided to check on their move there and asked a few questions, not about ghosts, but the apartment in general. They said they liked the size of it and the neighbors were great but some strange things were always happening, and they couldn't quite figure them out. The lights going on and off, shadows near the basement entrance and someone or something poking at them when they were asleep. This made June feel much better and she smiled all the way home. She wasn't imagining those frightening things after all.

After they made the move to yet another place on State Street, she soon found out that her life wasn't much better than at the old haunted apartment. The ghost was there too. Did he make the move with them?

Mirror, Mirror

June knows he is in the backroom off the bathroom. Once she was hit on the head by something she could not see . . . it left a bump the size of an egg on her forehead. Another time her nephew was shaving in the bathroom. His story follows:

"I saw him watching me in the bathroom mirror. He was an ugly old man with a bullet-like head and deep, dark eye sockets. His eyes seemed to burn into the mirror with a sort of consuming hatred. I was shaving at the time of his appearance and I felt a chill creep into my body. In a moment he would disappear, so I hoped. I was imagining things, that's all, I kept telling myself, but unfortunately I wasn't. I looked casually into the mirror before running out of the room and the old one was there grinning at me. I began running hell-for-leather down the street, half shaven at that. People stared, I didn't care, I only wanted to get a long way from that mirror, old man and apartment house. I was puffing

38

when at last I reached the restaurant where June worked.

"June asked, 'What's the matter? Something frighten you?'

"I didn't answer her right away, but she knew immediately that her house ghost had made another appearance. She said not to worry and gave me a wide, reassuring smile. 'It's all right, you relax,' June said. 'You've seen that nasty old man ghost of ours, haven't you? A nasty experience, a terrible shock but you're going to be all right. He's harmless but scary, I have to admit.'

"That night as I brushed my teeth I was afraid to look in the bathroom mirror and just as I feared when I did look, the face I saw was a familiar one . . . the toothless old ghost was grinning at me!"

Jarring Phone Calls

"I have never been frightened by ghosts or spirits but I've been bothered with them many times," says petite Lou, a gray-haired nurse from upstate New York.

Lou and her husband, Herb, loved foreign cars and always bought two of them at the same time; one was used solely for spare parts. These French imports had the damnedest maneuvering mechanisms; with one push of a red button on the dashboard, the car body would rise up several inches over the tires. That was for high-water days in Europe, Herb explained.

This couple always made an afternoon visit to Zuke who lived on the mucklands outside of town. Eating sour cherries and drinking Zuke's homemade cherry wine, made an enjoyable time for all. Late one evening, Lou and Herb made an unexpected appearance and Lou could not stop talking about her sister's funeral.

As Lou told her story, tears fell to her clothing, but she never stopped to dry them:

"The afternoon dragged on and on and I felt lonely. It was nearly three on the wall clock and now I would never again hear from my sister. I tried to think of more pleasant things, a new dress, the latest movie now playing or perhaps baking a lemon cake, it was her favorite. Then with tears in my eyes, I reached over and picked up my sister's photo and kissed it. That is when it all started to happen!"

"There was a slight tap at the front door, then the phone rang and when I rushed to answer it, no one was there, but I saw my sister walking down the walk. I saw her get into a car and drive down the road. I could not believe what I was seeing."

Evidently their dog also sensed something extraordinary going on, for it was found to be hiding under a table, acting quite strangely.

"Again my phone started to ring and for the next three minutes I could not get it to stop. For the next three weeks it rang exactly at 3 p.m. There was never a sound coming from the other end of the line."

Lou said for years she and her sister talked on the phone from three until four every afternoon. The two would talk over the day's events, their problems and sometimes just plain old family gossip.

For awhile all went well, then one morning Lou's mother died unexpectedly and another series of eerie events started happening in her life.

Though the knock seemed extremely loud, Lou didn't answer the door right away. After the second or third knock, she ran and had reached the front door when the phone rang. That startled her so badly that she snatched the door open before lifting the receiver. No one was outside. No one on the phone! Who had knocked? She was still inside the doorway when she saw the ghostly figure of her dead sister leaving the front steps. At about this same time, her mother's body was passing through the town for funeral services later in the week in upstate New York. Thoroughly frightened now, she turned and ran out of the house to her neighbor's to await Herb's arrival.

Later that evening when she had calmed down, her sister's spirit appeared in a weird cloud-like substance, near her bedside. Lou was amazed to be able to recognize her dead sister's features in that golden brightness. She had the presence of mind to ask her what the trouble was and the apparition whispered softly, "Lou,

Lou, don't worry about me, I'm all right. We don't die, it's just another plane our bodies go into. Mom is here too." And then she melted completely away.

Lou says her phone still rings at three o'clock in the afternoon on very special anniversaries and occasionally there's a knock on the door that doesn't sound quite normal, but now she just smiles and shrugs it off as another lovable spirit on the prowl.

Sara's Visit

Sitting in a comfortable chair in her office, the hour somewhat past midnight, nurse Lynn finally revealed her closely held secret to me. "All I really wanted," she said, "was a peaceful night."

Shortly after the late shift began, nurses start their bed checks. Lynn decided to pour herself a cup of coffee, leaving the other nurse alone to finish up. When the nurse retunred to Lynn's station they began talking about Sara, a former patient, and her midnight strolls. The two nurses then compared sightings and found Sara's spirit was coming to her old room and seemed to be happy with her only friends . . . the nurses at Mercy Hospital.

Sara had spent most of her life alone. Some years back Sara's relatives disowned her after she supposedly willed all her money and estate to the Humane Society. Now, since her hospital confinement, she spent many hours walking the halls and talking to the nurses. They all cared for her and loved her dearly.

Lynn gave Sara special attention, especially when brushing her long white hair. She wore it in a bun during the day and at night it flowed softly down her back. She always walked along the hallway in her long nightgown and the nurses offered her treats and hot tea which she enjoyed along with good conversation. These nurses were her family now and she loved them as much as they loved her.

Sara died in her sleep of natural causes and they all missed her nightly visits to the nurses' station. Her strolls up and down the hallway had made the evenings pass by a little faster for the late shift.

Shortly after Sara's burial, Lynn was turning out the lights along the hallway and getting ready for a quiet evening at her desk, when she thought she heard soft footsteps coming her way, but could see no one. She had left one light on at the nurses station and another at the other end of the hall, as was the practice for these late hour shifts.

Again footsteps and again no one in sight. Suddenly her eyes caught sight of a faint figure walking towards Sara's old room and then it disappeared. The figure had long white hair flowing softly behind her as she glided along the hallway.

At first Lynn wouldn't tell anyone but her husband Ken, a police officer, who didn't believe in such things. As an officer of the law, it was the live ones he worried about and he told her so in a kind way.

A few nights later the same eerie incident happened, and now Lynn knew for sure it was Sara. The hair so wispy and white, those piercing blue eyes and firmly set smile. "I'll be darned if it isn't old Sara herself," she whispered aloud. Lynn knew it was dear Sara's ghost on her nocturnal stroll through the hallway as she had done for years when she was alive. But she didn't dare tell her fellow workers, not right now anyway. One curious thing about Sara's ghost is that it appeared to open the door of the room into which she disappeared.

Then, one cold December night, shortly after the late shift nurses began their bed check, they heard sounds coming from Sara's empty room. Upon investigating they found no one, but Sara's favorite bed slippers were on the bedspread. How they got there, Lynn said, no one knows. All of Sara's belongings had been given away to the needy patients at the hospital after she had died.

Skeptics like to suggest that such episodes are the work of pranksters in the hospital hoping to frighten new nurses on the night shift.

One nurse said she often saw the spirits of dead relatives around the bedside of a patient who was on the point of death.

Lynn said, "I started working at the hospital without any pre-conceived notions about ghosts and spirits, especially in this place. That is until I met Sara."

Sara is still seen in that hospital wing and the nurses smile as she checks on them before returning to her lonely hospital room.

Moving Coffin

One of the first settlers was Grandfather Burnett, a mean old Frenchman who hated his wife, and was accused of mistreating her. She never complained but continued to obey his every command, raise their ten children, and during the tourist season, sell his carvings at the marketplace. This was their only means of income.

Week after week and month after month he fought with his wife. Now and then the quarrels would assume a bitter aspect, and threats were made by him in uncompromising language. He would go out drinking with the moonshiners and return home each time in a more angry and discontented frame of mind than before. Shortly before Grandmother Burnett became ill, there had been an argument exceeding in bitterness anything which had gone before. Again she didn't complain, but this time she said to her miserable husband, with a grim decision, "I'm coming back again, after I die, then you'll be afraid of me!"

That following summer, Grandmother died, and the family gathered at the homestead to say goodbye to their sweet, old "Grandmamee" as they called her. Grandfather was dressed in his finest and all his children watched him closely to see if he would feel any remorse or shed one tear. Of course, he didn't and they weren't surprised but felt rather outraged.

A year had lapsed after the funeral and the sadness of the family had worn away. The neighborhood had gone on its accustomed way, Grandfather still more revengeful than before his wife's death. As he began to relax, the fear of his wife coming back from the dead left his mind and he started looking for

43

another wife. Yes, at age 75!

Before he had time to start his courting, a storm came, flooding the island. Many lives were lost and property damage was extensive. But the most frightening thing was the uprooting of caskets from their shallow graves. The cemetery was a long distance from the Burnett farm so they weren't too concerned about dead bodies floating about.

That is until early one morning, after the flooding stopped, when Grandfather Burnett stepped off his back porch. There, resting near the bottom step was his wife's coffin, lid ajar with one of her skeleton arms stretched out toward him!

She had kept her word, as always.

She had at last come home to haunt him.

And haunt him she did for many years after this incident.

Angela said her parents often told this story about Grandfather Burnett's life after the second burial of Grandmother Burnett.

One night Grandfather sat alone in the kitchen of his old house. It had once been a cozy room when his wife was alive, but time and neglect had done their work and it was now little better than a cow barn.

He heard a noise as if someone was at the door and looked up. Then he called for whoever it was to come in, but there was no response. With a muttered blasphemy he kicked open the door and found no one there. He sank back at the kitchen table and poured himself a stiff drink . . . probably homemade wine from the wild grapes he so fondly collected from his backyard.

He was startled to see something standing before him like the battered form of his dead wife. For a few moments there came upon him a sort of fear. This was a new feeling for Burnett, nothing alive or dead could make him fearful. The specter before him had distorted features and glowing white eyes. She was inhuman —the only thing that seemed real, as when she was alive, was her long graying hair. She eyed her husband with a long, cold stare. He looked and began to realize the actuality of her presence, found the hatred of her which he had had for so many years, surging up again in his heart. All the brooding violence of the past year seemed to find a voice at once as he asked her, "Why are you here? You're dead and buried and for the second time!"

"I am here for no love of you, but because you now must know how much I suffered under your control," she said in so fierce a whisper that even Burnett was startled for an instant. Then his ghostly wife's distorted face broadened out in a ghastly attempt at a smile. It was hideous mockery, for the broken features and crinkled scars took strange shapes and queer lines of white showed out as the straining muscles pressed on the face.

"This is my way to warn you that your time is coming soon," and with a fierce gesture she backed out through the closed kitchen door and vanished into the darkness.

The next day the family found Grandfather looking deadly pale. He had a frightened look in his eyes. The harshness of his voice was gone.

From that day, there seemed some shadow over Grandfather Burnett, Angela explained. He neither ate nor slept as he had been accustomed, and his former habit of turning suddenly as though someone were stalking behind him, was gone too.

He no longer waited for his dead wife to appear. His face was a shocking sight that made all who saw it shudder, for there was on it a look of unutterable horror. Burnett cried to his children, "I have proof of my own eyes, I saw her and I watched her vanish through that door, but why is she doing this to me?"

He died a haunted man.

Teachers See Ghosts Too

Let me start out by telling you what one elderly teacher told me of her experiences with ghosts. I listened intently, knowing I was hearing stories true and unadorned.

"Had you known these old timers as long as I had, and heard their ghost stories, many relating similar experiences, you would believe in spirits and ghosts too, no matter how fantastic.

"The story teller in olden times was a respected, admired and much sought after individual. He or she was extremely talented in holding audiences spell-bound by manner, gestures, tone of voice and facial expressions, as well as by the content of the story. They also had remarkable memories.

"A number could foretell deaths as they often saw and recognized an apparition of a living person in his exact likeness just before death. My mother told of an incident where she was walking up the stairs and on the step ahead of her was Auntie's tulle veil. She was about to pick it up, when the phone rang. Her husband answered the phone, and then called to her, telling her it was long distance. She answered the call and her uncle cried out that his wife had just died! She rushed back to the stairway to pick up Auntie's veil but it was gone. Could it have been Auntie's farewell to them?

"I had a friend who, before dying, told me she would try to return not to scare anybody, but only to see her family again. She kept her word if later accounts can be believed. She has been seen at a distance from time to time, strolling across the lawn of her old homestead, sometimes being mistaken for a live woman.

"My grandmother told this story and we had no reason not to believe her because she didn't believe in ghosts. She suddenly sensed something in her living room. A dark patch of air formed around the teacup in her hand. After it disappeared she took a sip of the tea and was immediately sorry; her lips felt numb, then her tongue had a bitter, sticky taste. She believed that it was an evil spirit. These spirits can cause mischief even though they're not full-fledged apparitions."

Sweet Phantoms

"When I was a young girl of nine or ten, Mrs. Sweet, our housekeeper, asked me to pick blackberries with her on the nearby farm. I was alone in one section of the patch when I turned and watched the bramble moving. Then I saw it. Behind the bush, half-hidden by a swirl of mist, a grayish shape hovered. I was trying very hard to hide my terror from Mrs. Sweet who was afraid of her own shadow, but when the shape moved near my basket of berries, I screamed to the housekeeper, 'Ghost, ghost,' and took off for home. Mrs. Sweet was not far behind, yelling something and not making any sense at all.

"We reached home, breathless from the run. I thought after quite a long deliberation, it was probably all right to tell my mother, Angeline.

"The following evening, when we had finished an early supper, we gathered around the kitchen. 'I have a scary story to tell you . . . a short, true one.' When I had finished, my father explained that in some instances phantoms return in hopes of atoning for some wrong done in life. The apparition seemingly appeared not to fulfill a promise but to seek one. In appearance he was filmy or misty, unsubstantial, yet of natural color and blurred, but a distinct image. This ghost has been seen well into the twentieth century. I never forgot the incident, nor Dad's explanation, and I haven't eaten a blackberry in years!"

Her memory was so good, I had her tell me another story:

"As a child I had listened with great care to what our housekeeper's husband had said about the Civil War. He was Private Sweet and I had to hear about his battles almost daily. I can recall the whole conversation word for word about the Battle of Bull Run.

After the war, Pvt. Sweet retired to a small town along the Erie Canal and worked for a while on the New York Central Railroad. When President Lincoln's funeral train passed through his town, he stood proudly at attention on the train station platform and saluted his Commander-in-Chief for the last time.

To this very day, railroad crewmen working on the tracks have seen the phantom Lincoln funeral train pass by this same station with the flag-draped coffin visible and military guards in attention as if it were a live happening!

If you want to see this ghost funeral train, be at the New York Central tracks early in the morning and only during the month of April, says old Irlando, a retired railroad crewman, who boasts he has seen Lincoln's funeral train twice. No one can predict when it might appear again!

Around the Clock

There are several legends connected to this house on Spook Woods Road. One involves the story of an antique clock that has been broken for many years. It sits solemnly on the walnut mantel in the living room and the family enjoys its beauty and silence. Besides, they can't think of parting with it; it was an anniversary gift from their great-grandmother. It has both sentimental and monetary value of great importance.

It was eleven-thirty in the evening when Loretta saw the living room door open and then close. No one entered the room, yet she felt the presence of something strange and spooky. She closed her eyes trying to escape the cold, frightening feeling around her.

The antique clock started ticking! Loretta couldn't believe it. Suddenly the beauty surrounding the old time piece made her blink. An aura of pastel-colored light shone above the clock. It ticked away for several seconds, then stopped. The coldness in the room returned to its normal summer temperature, the old mantelpiece looked the same and Loretta shook her head in disbelief. Did this all happen or was she imaging it?

Loretta said they didn't believe in any sort or kind of ghost until they bought this house. Now she and her family have fully accepted the fact that they have unbidden guests and indeed would not be without them. After seventeen years, they feel their home is haunted by happy ghosts for they have never harmed anyone. When you hear a ghost walking up and down the stairway or across the floors in the middle of the night, it's hard to ignore.

One summer afternoon Loretta and her husband were in the living room when suddenly the Seth Thomas clock on the mantel started chiming. As explained, they had never heard a tick out of it! Their ghost seems to have a penchant for fooling around with timepieces. Loretta said that an old railroad pocket watch, broken for years, would start working for a few days, then stop until the ghostly incidents started up again.

Loretta thinks the ghost is Captain Bevier, who had been so

attached to the property that he can't let go. This ghost story is much neater if we assume it is the Captain wandering around the place, flickering the lights, rattling pans, starting clocks and generally upsetting the household. Loretta has traced the land upon which this house was built as far back as the early 1800s. The land was given to Captain Bevier during the Revolutionary War.

The one thing that really scares Loretta is the white cobweb that moves across the windows just before a ghostly event. Her next door neighbor says she has seen a shadow in the window facing this haunted house for many years now.

Many are the strange happenings in this lovely farmhouse, doors and windows that have been left open bang shut with great force and those that have been shut continually open by themselves. Objects move without human contact, unexplained appearances of articles and ghosts, and furniture moves up and down stairs at night and everyone is kept busy placing things back in their proper places.

Her son had a few scary moments, too. For one thing, he seems to pick up voices and noises in his stereo. Once he heard the breathing of someone coming through the speakers—he was home alone. Another time the smell of a strong odor was noticed coming from the stereo. Hours afterwards, he said, he experienced a "burning chill" on the spot where he thinks the ghost touched his sound equipment.

"Tuning in" is when we tune into spirits. It's like their feelings were our own, and could be the spirits' way of communicating. Loretta has heard the swish of clothing on the staircase just before the ghost appears; it has happened so many times, she now ignores the incidents. She will tell you there is nothing sinister about the ghostly presence and most family members regard it as a benevolent and friendly ghost, just as she does.

Whenever the cellar door opens slowly at midnight, followed by noises in the cellar, they usually just ride out these spooky times. But scrapings on the windows do get their attention. The peculiar difficulties can be turned to amusement, teased Loretta. "We are all ghost busters in my family!"

Is That You, Bruce?

It is difficult to disbelieve the words of local residents who come forth with their encounters with the unknown. Such stories of the unexplainable help to enrich an area's heritage but for reasons the author understands and respects, the exact location of this experience has not been revealed. However, most of the story is readily identifiable.

This family, who boasts an on-site specter, is utterly convinced of its existence, yet they are not the sort of people who would harbor dotty superstitions. These folks are solid as bedrock, pillars of a prosperous, picturesque community steeped in historical tradition. The story was related to me follows:

"We lived on this farm for several years and I have a good feeling about this house. I cannot believe that whoever might be in here with us would be harmful."

The family said they never particularly believed in ghosts, but always liked to read and tell good spook stories. It wasn't until they read the local ghost book of Port Byron that they began to feel there might be something to those kinds of stories.

"Bruce lived in this house with his second wife," she explained. "We didn't know the family and had never seen Bruce; he died shortly before our arrival back here. We did find a photo of him in the cellar; his wife must have forgotten it along with several other boxes of her things."

The first time they saw Bruce's spirit was in the early evening, when the two of them were watching television . . . she and her husband. To her left is the staircase which leads to the second floor. Suddenly she felt someone was looking over her shoulder. She slowly turned her head toward the stairway and her eyes were led to the top of the steps. To her shock there was the figure of a man standing there; it was like a solid figure. She couldn't make out any facial features from that distance, but he was dressed in work clothes and boots. Her immediate reaction was that it was Bruce. He was a farmer, and that's the way he would have been dressed. As if to check her vision, she turned away for an instant and looked up to the top step again but the figure had vanished.

I asked her if the ghost was a whitish apparition or smoky figure and she answered, "Neither. It is a life-like image of Bruce. In fact he looks very much like the picture we still have in our cellar."

They have seen Bruce several times since. He looks very human and has a smile on his face. He always comes up from the cellar, walks past the TV screen, then up the stairs he goes with his feet floating several inches above the steps. He never comes back down and that puzzles them. It is the same route every time and happens at least twice a week.

Her husband then joined in on the conversation and said that it doesn't bother them anymore. Whenever Bruce's ghost comes in front of the TV screen, they just sit perfectly still and watch him slowly move out of the room.

Exasperated and amazed, but again not particularly frightened, they simply spoke to Bruce's spirit one night as he passed in front of their screen. "All right. If you want to live with us, that's fine, but please keep the doors shut."

On another occasion, she was watching television alone in the living room, when she felt a very cold breeze and saw the clear figure of a man brushing past her. She gave it no thought, believing that it was her husband. The figure disappeared as it climbed up the stairs. She got up from her chair and walked to the foot of the stairs to talk to him, but he was not there. Then she heard her husband coming in the back door. When she related the happenings of the previous few minutes, he swore he hadn't been in the house for quite some time.

Spirited Mother-in-Law

During the darkest hours of the night, Marion was awakened by what she afterwards described as an exceedingly hard slap upon her cheek. She leaped off the bed and saw the upper half of a woman's body drifting away from the room, where it disappeared through the closed door.

She rushed out to tell her family that she had a terrible experience. Before she could say a word, her daughter called out from her bedroom; she too had a bad experience. When they compared tales, both mother and daughter had almost identical ordeals. It was Marion's mother-in-law's ghost teasing them. Her ghost will often appear, knock over a cup, shut a door in their faces just as they are about to enter a room, and cause them many sleepless nights with her manifestations.

Once, provoked by the continuous silence of the family, the ghost threw a coffee cup. It hit the cupboard door solidly, but didn't break. Another spooky incident, Marion reported, was that her dinner plates were seen floating about the kitchen and then they all settled down in their rightful places on the table, including the extra place where her mother-in-law always sat.

Funny, but Marion says the ghost has never appeared to her husband, the ghost's son. Although he has frequently heard the sound of her voice echoing from the lower part of the house and sometimes also hears the faint peal of her cold, unnatural laugh.

Late one evening Marion watched as the woman's figure slowly and sadly glided away in a gleam of light that made her shield her eyes with her hand. When she looked again, the ghostly figure had vanished.

Many objects have been moved mysteriously while they are asleep, and Marion knows it's her mother-in-law's spirit wandering about the house as she often did when she was alive. "She was a night walker then and she's a night haunt now," Marion said.

They treat the odd goings-on with a playful benevolence but others visiting them have been genuinely frightened by her ghost. The family is used to their spirited mother-in-law!

Ghosts Do Exist

Dick's mother-in-law said she awoke with a dreadful feeling of suffocation; cold perspiration stood on her forehead, and she could hardly draw a breath. There was a lead-like weight on her chest. She tried to cry out but her voice was gone.

Suddenly she saw a ghostly figure walking away from her bed and disappear into the wall without a sound.

She went downstairs and let out an appalling scream. Her family rushed to her side and between cries and screams, she told them of her frightening experience.

"I saw something," she told Dickie, "that made my skin prickle with goose bumps. It made me so afraid that I am not going to sleep in that room by myself anymore. I'm not one to be afraid of anything like that, ever, but I just saw something ghostly. It was like something flying in the air, like a shadow. It looked at me for a second, and then it was gone."

"We were all aware of strange happenings," Dickie said. "Once there was a banging sound on the outside of the house. We looked all around the yard, inside the garage and porches, but found no one.

"Objects would mysteriously fall off shelves when I was in the room alone, especially in the kitchen and I would have to catch the object before it hit the floor. I didn't feel afraid; I felt annoyed. I never saw the ghost, but many times I'd turn my head and catch this sort of shadow effect."

Dickie has constantly heard doors closing and lights flicking on and off. There can be no doubt that the experiences of his mother so terrified the family that they refused to leave her alone.

As Dickie reports, "One night the spirit or whatever it was that seemed to be haunting them was late in coming. His mother was already asleep, just as his mother-in-law had been. Suddenly she was awakened by the pressure of a heavy hand on her head and a hot breath so close it seemed as if someone were right next to her. No one was around; no one visible to her anyway.

Then a hasty withdrawal of the pressure, and the sound of footsteps—heavy—retreating through the darkness to the further end of her bedroom.

She screamed out for help and rushed into the nearby bathroom, where she locked herself in until the family came to her rescue. A thorough search of the house revealed nothing unusual.

Even the animals were asleep in their assigned places.

She then came to believe that the whole affair was the outcome of one of those very vivid dreams which sometimes come to us in the semi-conscious moment between sleep and waking.

On another night, although she was still not sure about the breathing, she was quite certain about the heavy pressure upon her head and chest, then the footsteps distinctly moving away from her bed towards the door. They did not reach the hallway but stopped half-way and were heard no more. For some seconds she stood without moving. Her eyes dropped slowly from the bed to the floor. She trembled with fear as she heard the footsteps start to move across the room again. The door was literally opening to allow something out. She could feel the difference in the room's temperature; the air was cold now. She listened, and now she could hear new ghostly sounds flowing through the hallway. Sounds came from the bathroom, but she was too frightened to leave her bed, instead she pulled the covers over her head and waited until dawn before telling her family of her nightmare. Or was it?

Susan, My Hats!

Susan leaned close to me at a recent Democratic dinner benefit and whispered, "I believe in ghosts . . . I have had the strangest experience recently. Our house is haunted, you know."

With this beginning, I knew this political fund raiser was going to be anything but dull.

Susan and her family bought an old home in Owasco. When the former owners moved off the farm to another home down the road a ways, they left behind many of their possessions in the attic. No one touched them for months, thinking some member of the family would come back for the junk, as Susan called it. She didn't even know what was up there . . . many boxes . . . some still unopened.

One warm summer day, Susan decided to clean the attic and

return the most valuable items to the family . . . fishing poles, china, really nothing worth saving but it belonged to them and she didn't dare throw it away. The old couple, now happy in their new home, didn't seem too excited about their stuff being returned, but Susan left it anyway.

A few weeks later the old woman died and they were all sad that she didn't live longer in her new home. According to the neighbors, the great Maude was a very meticulous woman and took great pride in her home and her appearance. Indeed, her friends had been known to comment, "She was a lady of many outfits with matching hats."

Several months later, when Susan started cleaning the attic and preparing it for a good paint job, she heard a noise that seemed to come from the farthest corner of the room. When she peered into the darkness, she saw nothing. An empty attic can be eerie, but Susan had bright plans for it and dismissed all unpleasant thoughts.

The east corner was so dark she had to feel her way around the walls to get to it. She was suddenly shocked and surprised to find a large box hidden there. How did they miss it?

Pulling the cardboard box out into the open light, she was astonished to see it full of beautiful, fancy hats. As she started to carry it through the attic doorway, it jumped about a foot into the air and landed on its side. As quickly as she righted it, Susan claimed, the box jumped again. She remained calm because she had never given much credence to what she called "psychic" stuff, but she knew something strange was going on in this house.

When she opened the faded hat box for her family later that night, they knew immediately they were Maude's hats. They had seen pictures of Maude wearing some of them in the photos they had taken back to the family.

What to do with them now that Maude was dead? She knew that her husband and children didn't want them. In fact, they emphasized that on her last delivery to them that if they found anything else it could be given away or thrown out.

But the hats were too lovely to throw away, Susan argued to her husband. Perhaps some school theater group could use them or a church thrift shop could find a good home for them. Someone would be either keeping them for history's sake or use them on stage someday, she hoped.

The next day, Susan loaded up the lovely hats and took them to a church garage sale and was happy to get rid of them. After she left the hats, she felt the uncomfortable sensation of someone watching her as she drove home along the lonely back roads.

That night her sleep was troubled by a slight breeze brushing her face. Then she was startled out of a deep sleep by a voice whispering, "Susan, my hats, my hats." She sat up with a jerk, then listening, she distinctly heard the same voice, "Susan, my hats, my hats." It seemed to come from the attic again, as before, the words were repeated softly, "My hats, Susan, my hats."

Susan was not afraid, merely curious, but was glad of the light she had turned on. "John did you hear that voice?"

Her husband is a no-nonsense school teacher who had acquired the house and land for a reasonable price and he was well pleased with his bargain. He was not disposed to believe phenomena that could reasonably be written off as sounds to which many old houses are naturally prone.

But on this night when Susan shook him from a sound sleep to listen to the spirited voice, his comfortable rationale began to slip. They both knew that there was no physical being in the room, but most definitely felt the very strong sensation of an icy breeze pass their heads as the voice called out, "My hats, my hats."

Could the dead Maude still be in their house?

Susan told her daughter Katie that she believed that there was a spirit in her bedroom last night. Katie wasn't at all surprised. She told her mother, "Some time in the middle of the night, something passed by and bumped my head."

Susan and her family fully accept the fact that they have an unbidden guest and indeed would not be without her, for they feel that their home is haunted by a happy ghost, as such a charming home should be.

"This is Maude's home," Susan says. "She doesn't make us too uncomfortable. We rather enjoy our ghost and are reluctant to do anything that might annoy her."

Horse and Buggy Vision

One windy night, Sam went outside to shut the shutters on his house. As he struggled with the windows, he briefly caught a glimpse of a horse and buggy coming down the road from the direction of his neighbor's house on the hill.

When it had passed, the driver waved and Sam waved back but there was something strange about this scene. The horse and buggy seemed to be floating a few feet above the dirt road and were noiseless, not a sound coming from the wagon wheels.

Sam told his wife, who was waiting inside for him, that Jim had just passed by coming from his house and heading towards the highbridge. She looked shocked and cried, "It can't be."

Sam answered, "Yes, I know, but it was Jim and his rig."

They both agreed that it was Jim's spirit returning to the scene of his tragic death. Jim had drowned in the Erie Canal earlier that month. His horse was spooked by a milk wagon on the towpath road and both Jim and his rig fell into the water. Jim couldn't swim but made a valiant attempt to hold onto the leather lines attached to his horse. Soon the horse went under and Jim struggled to stay with his wooden wagon until help arrived. The men on the canal bank threw him a tow rope and they thought he had it, but mistakenly he was holding on to the reins from his horse.

He drowned under the mucky waters right before the crowd and his young son. Minutes later they got to him but it was too late—Jim was dead.

Local farmers around the Towpath settlement say on some still nights, they can hear the hooves of Jim's horse and the wagon wheels clinking as he drives along the Erie.

Black Ghosts

An eighteenth century house, eerie and isolated but perfectly preserved and occupied by a devout Catholic family, is haunted by black ghosts.

This house was built at the period when slavery was about to end in the deep south. Wendy, who did a title search for the family, says their home was known to have been a stop for the Underground Railroad, although some of these refuges for escaped slaves were not recorded in history.

A legend tells of ghostly horses, hooves thundering past their home on certain nights of the year. All this Wendy says is still part of their daily lives in this haunted house.

This family have ghosts who have lived with them for many, many years, and they "talk." Yes, they will pat Wendy's dad on the shoulder and say "Sit down, John," and gently push him into his favorite chair.

Wendy's mom said, "You'll walk through the kitchen and there will be nobody there, and you'll see a chair pulled out from the table, you'll push it in, come back and the chair will be pulled out again."

Among other apparitions reported is that of a black man who runs up and down the hall. Some of the spooky ambience seems to come with the territory. During the Civil War, there were hidden rooms in the house with tunnels under the cellar which are now sealed off. The story goes that black slaves were kept there until they could be safely moved to another area. The New York Central Railroad runs north of the house and was used to transport them out of town.

Wendy tells of an experience that seems typical of the sort of anecdotes her grandmother tells involving their nightly visitations. Grandmother seems to have the most trouble with these ghosts. Every night a ghost will ask for a drink of water. She then has to go downstairs and bring up a glass of water, set it on the night stand and go back to bed. If she doesn't do it, the ghost will bother her all night long. Now this has been going on for over thirty years. Recently on one of her night trips, around two a.m., she felt two bony hands on her shoulders. Twisting sharply around, she saw a black ghost standing close behind her. It seemed to be human in shape but very, very short, the eyes were like two black holes. When she reached the kitchen door, the ghost disappeared through the cellarway. This cellarway is the scene of many unusual noises and the door is found open at all hours of the day or night. It has no less than four locks on it.

As with so many haunted houses, there are convincing reports of unexplained footsteps. But with these noises are not only footsteps, but muttering voices nearly every night.

One evening the family sat round the kitchen table talking about school affairs when faint raps, rapidly increasing in loudness, were heard apparently coming from the walls in various parts of the house. On entering a room, they would switch on a light and the noises would cease but resume when the light went off again. When the mother began to read prayers from the Bible, the rapping noises became quieter and stopped.

Another time, Wendy was sitting in the haunted kitchen and all of a sudden out of the corner of her eye, she looked at the cellar door and caught part of a black figure. It never fully materialized but she could feel its presence in the room.

The consensus is that the black ghosts were escaped slaves who probably never made it out of town and are now buried somewhere on the property.

There is one secret room built into the kitchen chimney, reached by a concealed stairway where it is believed they hid the runaway slaves. The door was bricked up and remained so for over a century. That is until unaccountable sighs and groans were frequently heard behind the bricks. The present owners decided to open doorway. What they found remains a family secret.

Haunted Shoes

When Cousin Mary passed away, her children said to Liza's mother, "Come get Mom's black patent leather shoes. She always wanted you to have them."

But Liza's mother was afraid of dead people and refused to even go to the funeral, say nothing of wearing her dead cousin's shoes!

Days went by, and finally her husband asked her to go get them before someone else did and she replied, "Let them have those black shoes and with my blessings!"

That night, Cousin Mary's spirit came to her in a dream and was carrying the shoes. She came over to the bed and threw the shoes on the covers and said, "Here I brought you my shoes. Now wear them!"

Early the next morning Liza's mother told her seventeen children to stay in the yard because she had to make a call at Cousin Mary's house.

Her mom came home with the shiny black shoes and put them on the stand near her bed.

Her husband was shocked. "Why the shoes now?" he asked. Then she told him about cousin Mary coming to her in a dream. "Maybe now she won't bother me anymore. Here are her shoes and I hope she is happy."

And she never did appear again to Liza's mom or to any other member of the family.

Moving Ghost

Years ago tall, grey-haired Joe told this story about a "moving ghost" that haunted a house in Auburn.

All traces of this haunted house have now disappeared and its site has been occupied by a succession of buildings, but none of them can boast a ghost as fearful as that which moved from room to room, terrifying not only the local residents but out-of-towners as well.

This house looked haunted the day it was built. It did not acquire a reputation for ghostly manifestations until after 1910 when a member of the household is said to have died under rather suspicious circumstances.

The tale begins with a news report that this house was inhabited by a "moving ghost." Its nature was not quite clear from the garbled accounts of those who had the misfortune of seeing it.

Among the many unsubstantiated but persistent stories associated with the building, is the account of the landlord's uncle who spent a night in the house, carrying a loaded shotgun. He later reported that during the night, he fired at an entity that leaped at him from the fieldstone fireplace. He heard a loud thud and it disappeared into the darkness of the chimney.

Ghostly footsteps at night are reported to have frightened the owners into moving out and leaving all their possessions. The whole house seemed to be trembling from the ghost's movements.

This ghost is said to have been seen clinging to a window ledge and screaming. Some spoke of a spectral woman who would rise from the wood floors at midnight and a voice crying out, "Move, move, or die." The voice fading away on the last word.

The last landlord of this spooky building said that the ghost caused at least one death, and possibly more, by heart attack. The victim was a tenant who dared to attempt to sleep by the fireplace on a cold wintery night.

Moon Shadows

This phantom dog was seen by many people as they passed the old haunted house. Once the then occupant of the house felt the dog touching him on his leg as the ghostly creature floated by him in the cold, dark hallway. For hours afterwards he felt a burning sensation all over his body.

Whether the residents of Auburn had been imagining things, seeing visions or not, one thing was certain, nothing on earth would induce any one of them to spend a night there.

That is until Joe, a local farmer known for his skill and courage, was told of the shadow of a ghost seen on a full moon night roaming from room to room. He immediately took the next trolley out of town to visit this haunted house.

An adventurer who was in the habit of tapping his pipe thoughtfully against the palm of his hand, Joe offered to spend a night in the house for a small fee. Accordingly, he went at dusk to the deserted building taking only his coffee jar, cigarettes, Prince Albert and a pint of whiskey to keep the chill away. By now the owner was anxious for a solution to the ghost problem and gave Joe his full cooperation.

Joe circled the house, and examined all doors and windows, then went into the house, taking a bat and flashlight with him.

The last of daylight died and the moon rose and began its passage across the skies. There was no sound but the townspeople gathered in the street hoping to catch a glimpse of the ghost. It was a Sunday evening and Joe found himself inside the fearful-looking and dilapidated vacant house. He decided to look over the house one more time and went from room to room with his trusty ballbat and flashlight.

The plaster had fallen in great lumps from the ceilings and walls and was scattered all over the place. He found himself talking to himself in whispers as he climbed the narrow staircase to the upper floor. The house was uninhabited and yet plainly someone or something had recently been there. Nothing that he could see or feel or know, but it was there, in the darkness. Joe also knew that during prohibition days the house was a favorite haunt of bootleggers and smugglers and it is thought that a horror story was invented perhaps to keep neighbors away from it.

He also believed that he could frighten himself into anything by thinking too much about the supernatural. He lit a cigarette and prepared to wait out the night.

The hours passed slowly by.

For the first time in his life, he was suddenly, icily afraid. He thought he saw a vague, shadowy figure next to him without a head, but he blinked and it was gone.

Suddenly the stair creaked quite plainly, and then another creak. After that the door latch began to move and a figure in white began to creep along the wall. Then a bumping and clicking sound in the hallway.

Joe looked up and standing before him in a patch of moonlight was a shapeless mass of shadows. He regarded them without flinching. He straightened his back, fixed his eyes on the glowing cigarette and prepared to ignore these ghostly images. Soon the shadows dissolved in the air and he was left alone in the dark empty house.

The apparitions always faded away at dawn.

In the morning Joe left the place and was convinced it was only the moonlight passing through the windows from room to room, casting shadows resembling human-like figures and nothing more!

No spirit or ghost to report.

The ghost-watchers on the street told Joe that nothing would ever convince them that it was only "moon shadows." And no explanation was ever discovered to satisfy the owner.

The Floating Alphabet

Louie said thoughtfully, "Here's something that might possibly be of interest to you. My last name is Rood which means 'crucifix' and for some unknown reason things happen to me that are unbelievable. I keep telling my mom of incidents that happened when I was younger and she says they didn't—only a dream. But I am awake when I have those thoughts and feelings of familiar places and people. It is all very real to me and I know this is my second time around!

"I take most of this quite calmly. It can be irksome, but is does in a way encourage me, for it indicates there really is a paranormal—that I have spirit companions.

"Once when I was around fifteen years old, I saw something very strange outside my bedroom door. We lived on Howlett Hill in Marcellus, my parents, sisters and I. It was midnight or later and I was in bed looking out the door into the hallway. Suddenly letters from the alphabet started floating, as if in water, by my room. They weren't in a straight line, but sort of a zigzagging formation. I was lying there trying to figure out this strange happening when I saw them pass again in the opposite direction. I quickly crawled under the covers.

"When I peeked out, it was over and I didn't know what to do. At first, I thought it was my sisters playing a trick on me. Then I realized they were asleep and there wasn't a sound coming from anywhere in the house. There was a creepy stillness about. Terrified, I ran out of my bedroom to the hallway, but found nothing. I realized then and there it was not a dream because I wasn't asleep.

"Ghostly letters in the dark hallway, spelling out a message. I am sorry I hid under the covers! Someone was trying to communicate with me. After all, this house is believed to have many ghosts."

The Valley of the Moon

Not far from town, in this beautiful and wild countryside, there is a romantic valley that has been almost unchanged for hundreds of years. You won't find the name on any map, but Port Byron residents can direct you to it. This spot is known as "The Valley of the Moon."

The most popular route to this valley is across the dam above Warren's Mill. Most parents worry about their children taking this route because the water is deep in the old raceway that once ran the mill wheel. Beyond the spillway is a well-worn path that goes along the top of the dam, past the foundry and the town dump, and across another bridge over a spillway at the west end of the dam. After climbing a hill it is possible to walk along a ridge on the west side of the millpond, an area fondly believed to be an old Indian trail. Histories say there was once an Indian path along the Owasco Outlet from Auburn to the Seneca River; the story seems to have been handed down from one generation to the next.

An easier trip to this mysterious valley is by Halsey Road. Travel south from about one quarter of a mile and look southeast; the valley will greet you with its enchanted beauty.

I should mention here that a recent visit to the romantic woods, misty outlet and rolling hills, inspired me to write this tale of the Moon Witch. This valley is an ideal location for ghost stories. As mauve and salmon sunsets softened these hills, the residents of years ago whispered dark tales of the white witch of the Valley of the Moon. She is said to have been seen in the vicinity of the outlet wandering among the trees on moonlit nights.

Behind the town, where wooded hills rise steeply, the witch's cottage once stood. It sat like a tiara on the hilltop overlooking the outlet. It seems to have had a bad reputation as far back as the early settlement of the town.

Children and grownups visiting or picnicking at the valley said that an old hag would come out on the porch and chase them away. One victim of an outburst of the witch's wrath was a young farm boy who foolishly threw a stone at her moss-covered wooden door. For a moment he simply held his breath and watched the "wild one" as she effortlessly yanked a sapling from the ground and hurled it at him.

People often showed no respect for the witch's property. Finally, according to the legend, she pronounced a curse on the town and its inhabitants. After that, they said, anyone who was sighted by the witch suffered for it.

Doris, my classmate said that almost everyone agrees that there is a strange atmosphere in the Valley of the Moon. The closest neighbors said that for many years the witch had been quite mad.

She had her animals chained to a specially built post to protect her from trespassers. She would watch, as her dogs howled far into the night, laughing fiendishly from her porch. These goings on did not sit well with the townspeople, who were all aware of her power.

Many years ago the witch, who dealt in wizardry, called at a neighbor's house but received a brusque welcome from the husband who chanced to open the door. He slammed it shut in her face. In revenge the spiteful witch resorted to witchcraft and, returning there in the dead of night, bound all the animals in the barn. On certain nights of the year, her ghost is said to have returned to the barn to repeat her wicked deed.

Stories of this witch, sometimes garbled, often contradictory and always frightening, were enough to keep the villagers from leaving their homes on full moon nights. When absolutely necessary to travel, they carried salt in their pockets as a protection against her. (Salt derived its power from its incorruptibility.) It also was placed in the cradle of newborn babies until they could be baptized. Another protection was strong iron in the form of a horseshoe—a symbol of the powerful worker, the smith. The horseshoe was hung, horns up, over doorways.

Preternaturally wise in matters of the season and soil, she always planted her seeds by the light of the moon. To her neighbors her lunar learnings didn't look logical but she always had a bountiful harvest.

Tales told that she danced by the light of the moon and this terrified them all. They tried repeatedly to catch her, but they never even came close to seeing the moon witch.

Merry Meet

An elderly lady told me of how she thought her grandfather had once walked with the ghostly witch of the Valley of the Moon.

It was a calm night and the fisherman walked along the Owasco Outlet in a happy mood. Suddenly, there was a loud cry in the field bordering his path. At first he supposed that a pack of hunting dogs was chasing a deer and then, as the sounds faded as suddenly as they had arisen, a spectral old hag chuckling and chortling appeared before him. He almost sprang from his hip boots. She tired to lure him to her wooded valley hideout to which, many believed, there was no escape. As the moon lit up the scene, he now saw that it was for sure the ugly valley witch, bristling all over with black shaggy hair, lame in one foot. Although he quickened his pace, he could not lose her. She accompanied him until he reached Halsey Road.

As he approached his parked truck, the witch turned and he found himself looking into her ghostly wrinkled face. Her eyes glared as if in anger or distress. She quickly mumbled some strange words over the frightened fisherman as she moved with gliding steps toward the valley's tall pines.

Exhausted physically and emotionally, he now discovered to his horror, that he could not move his feet. Half numbed from fright, he closed his eyes hoping she would disappear but instead he soon found himself seated in his truck! He never had the chance to open the truck door!

Afterwards he heard many tales of witchcraft being practiced in the valley area. Whenever anyone expressed disbelief of the witch of the Valley of the Moon, this fisherman would shake his head and aim them toward the outlet and say, "Go fishin' thar some moonlit night!"

One day her decaying cottage burned, and she supposedly died in the fire. Even in death, it was rumored that her evil magic was considered so strong that eventually a priestess was hired to cast a spell on the valley to keep her spirit in the ground.

Glancing toward the towering trees that cast uneasy shadows on the fields, old timers today watch the sunset colors deepen and whisper, "On nights when the moon is full, they say the ghostly witch still dances in the fields of the Valley of the Moon, wearing a shimmering white dress, cackling in her high-pitched voice."

If by chance you ever cross the enchanted valley and have the good fortune to experience some strange witch happening, don't be afraid. Just call out "Merry Meet," the proper witch greeting.

Who's That Knocking at My Door?

I have tumbled upon one of the most peculiar cases of haunting or devilment of some sort that I have ever heard of.

Ghosts are not necessarily evil. They can be good friends to mortals, so I have heard from many old timers. The ghosts ask only that you believe in their existence, that you do not scoff, that you treat them as equals though you live in different worlds. They can be good and true friends, and Cindy has proof of this from her experiences with dear Uncle Dale's spirit.

This ghost seems to try to be helpful.

It was three o'clock in the morning when Cindy and her two sons were awakened to the sounds of loud banging noises on the cellar door. It was an awful racket. They rushed to the basement, turned on the light and saw that there was no one, but the room was full of natural gas. Bummy, Cindy's dad, is convinced that the ghost's knocking saved his family and so are some members of the fire department emergency squad. Another few seconds and they would have all perished!

Several nights later, there was again a knocking at the cellar door. When they flung it open, there were strange noises, a mysterious cold draft and then a glimpse of the ghostly form of Uncle Dale.

Most of the ghosts reported in our area can be connected with some person who died here. Uncle Dale had died many years earlier in a car accident.

His ghost is considered a symbol of good luck. This popular ghost is very dignified, never moans or shrieks, doesn't rattle chains, and appears most of the time as a soft white glow which can be seen floating from room to room. Sometimes he moves slowly from one end of the house and disappears into the door on the other side. He also fades away if you get too close to him. Not everyone can see the ghost; sometimes the children have felt someone gently push them. Once ghostly hands gave them some friendly pats on their backs.

A neighbor once encountered an invisible presence half-way up Cindy's stairs, something that made it impossible to proceed. Whatever it was on the stairway that sunny afternoon, it stopped her in her tracks and she had no choice but to retreat. After a while she made another attempt to climb the stairs, and this time no presence visible or invisible barred her way.

What really started people thinking about Uncle Dale was the story of the bumble bee. After his death, his wife found a long red-haired bumble bee in her car. She knew it was her husband's spirit because Dale had red hair too. It followed her everywhere! One day it flew into her car as she started to leave for town. After the short trip to the store and home again, she opened the car door and the long-haired bee flew out and waited at the screen door for her. Once inside the bee flew to the top of the curtain above the sink and rested until she left the room. The bee stayed three days and then disappeared into the nearby cemetery. No one dared to kill the red bee. They knew it was Dale because it flipped its wings at anyone who called out his name!

Both Cindy and her aunt have had separate experiences in the old house. Both believe the presence there is Dale. "I have a very good feeling about this house," Cindy says, "and I cannot believe that this ghost or whatever might be in here with us, would be harmful." Cindy bought the house from her aunt shortly after this next incident.

Grandmother Elsie was one person who didn't appreciate this ghost's tricks. Every time she sat in Dale's rocking chair, it flipped over and she landed on the floor. At first she accused her sister (Dale's wife) of doing it and threatened to flatten her the next time it happened. But when Elsie was alone in the room and she flipped again, she knew it was the ghost. Elsie would yell out "That's that blessed Dale's spirit!"

Cindy rather enjoys the presence of her uncle. He is mischievous at times, but he has been a true friend and one who seems to be taking care of her and her children.

Michael, Cindy's son, loves this story of their ghost.

One day he and his friend Jason were playing in the upstairs hallway when suddenly Jason started falling down the many steps. Mysteriously he was swiftly lifted into the air and stayed suspended—his feet high above his head! Someone was holding him there in mid-air, yet they couldn't see anyone. Young Jason wasn't crying, but sort of giggling. Cindy and Jason's mother came running to help and when they saw Jason in the air, upside down, they froze. Cindy far from being frightened or upset, told them not to get too close or Uncle Dale's ghost would fade away and Jason could get hurt. Within a few seconds Jason was standing on his two feet again—still looking upward at the someone who had broken his fall.

Although the story sounds utterly fantastic, there may be more truth in it than anyone would like to believe. This family has no reason to make up these stories. Cindy said recently that her uncle's ghost "pops up all over the place at any time of the day or night." Although it is sometimes disconcerting when the ghost appears to walk through walls, it never troubles her, and in fact, it adds to the fun of living in this house. The down-to-earth Cindy stated that she enjoys the experience and rather hopes that the ghost never leaves. She feels very safe.

Uncle Dale's ghost made a habit of shaking her every morning to make sure she got up in time for work, but thoughtfully let her sleep late on the weekends. Every house could use a spirit as thoughtful and charming as this spooky old uncle.

The Ghost of Perkins

Often a house comes to be known as haunted because the people living there are open to such phenomena; they're psychic and are aware of what is going on in the space around them. Michele is such a person.

Her parents owned this lovely estate for many years. The house, in the Greek revival style, has many rooms beautifully decorated with family antiques—most engagingly and tastefully furnished. The grounds include wooded acres surrounded by tall dogwood trees and a hill behind the house and studio-barn. It is well-known as the Perkins home located on Main Street, near the old Erie Canal. Main Street is quaint and very attractive, lined with historical houses.

A little is known about Mr. Perkins. He was the village's first postmaster in 1824. He made violins in his workshop behind the house and violin patterns from wood. Reporter Irene, now ninety years old, recalls that Peter Kurtz, a well-known violinist, played a Perkins violin at a concert in London. This may be why violin music is heard late at night coming from the barn where he made his patterns and instruments.

Michele is a very interesting and highly intelligent lady and she states that she and her family have all seen the thin, tall, ghostly figure of Perkins from time to time, walking the halls after midnight, always checking the bedroom doors as he passes by. It is his nightly check and he very seldom misses his ghostly beat!

Michele says growing up in the Perkins house was a lovely but eerie experience. She says she immediately became aware of a presence. "I would feel cold pressure, accompanied by a door closing or opening. I would feel that something was there, watching. I was not afraid. I felt that this person was looking to see what I was doing, to see whether they should approve or not.

"I was sure that Mr. Perkins, the former owner who built this home, was around to make sure we were sincere in our efforts to restore the buildings," Michele explained.

She recalls instances that occurred during her teens. "Sometimes," she said, "we'd be in the kitchen and the doorbell would ring and we'd go to the door and there would be nobody there. This occurred around the clock but most often after midnight."

Nick, Michele's father, a teacher at the Central School, says that whenever the light would flicker, he'd yell out, "Oh, stop it," and the light would stay on.

There have been a number of other manifestations there. When Nick found the books off the library shelves, he at first blamed the children. But one night he left his bedroom and started to go downstairs when all of a sudden he heard books hit the floor. As he stepped onto the last step, it creaked and a figure surrounded by a light blue aura, floated up the stairs. It turned to him, smiled and continued on up and disappeared. He believes it was Mr. Perkins whom he recognized from a portrait in the house.

Why this ghost appears no one really knows, but with the house's history and its historic past, one might imagine almost anything could happen.

The Bonnie Story

The residence on South Street has been the scene of remarkable and unexplained happenings for many a full moon. As Bonnie explains, "We had an unidentified ghost living with us who could not find peace; his footsteps plagued us nightly, usually followed by a gust of icy cold air. We knew nothing about the ghost when we moved into the house. We were just looking for a home in the Port Byron school district."

This house had a long reputation for having a constant turnover of tenants before Bonnie arrived. It is interesting to note that this house and the few older ones in this part of town are located across from the Pine Hill Cemetery. It is reported that many of these houses have been plagued with alleged psychic disturbances dating as far back as the late eighteen hundreds.

This case is significant in the study of "ghost busting" because it involves the rare combination of apparitions and poltergeist manifestations.

Bonnie is convinced that the haunted house is full of ghosts and they come in all shapes and sizes; their presence has been felt daily. "I was in the kitchen when the apparition first appeared in a doorway," said Bonnie. "I thought it was one of my new neighbors and said to come in, but in an instant I knew better. There was something filmy about it and when I started to check it out more closely, it disappeared at once."

"Our ghost may be a female," says Bonnie, "because she loves to bother me when I am working in the kitchen." This spirit, in Bonnie's home must have had a special talent for cooking, especially with eggs. One incident in particular kept Bonnie genuinely puzzled. It seems that when she would put eggs on the table and leave the room, if only for a second, the eggs would disappear and somehow be back in the refrigerator. After several of these mischievous acts, Bonnie would yell out to the ghost, "Leave the eggs alone!" and without any warning a cup or dish would fly across the room.

There were other witnesses to this paranormal behavior including Marion, Bonnie's mom, two special friends and her brother-in-law, who refuses to spend any time in that haunted house with or without Bonnie. He is the one who heard voices of children playing upstairs late one afternoon when he was lying on the sofa trying to take a nap. He thought the family had gone to the movies and he was home alone, but suddenly he was awakened by loud laughter, screams and the rattling of chains. He decided that Bonnie must have changed her mind and left the children home. When she returned, he complained that he never in his whole life heard such a racket coming from upstairs. "I think your kids were playing war games all afternoon," he said. She looked startled and said, "You were alone. The kids were with me all day." He did a flip backwards off the sofa and rushed out of the house. Bonnie tried to explain that their ghost was good-humored and harmless, but he never heard a word she said. He was too busy listening to his heart pounding with fear as he fled her home for the last time.

"Over the years, we have heard something moving across the upstairs floors, fast, regularly, sounding like marbles rolling about." Some of her friends say it is the ghost of a little kid playing marbles back and forth across the rooms.

Twice, Bonnie says, something touched her on the shoulder as she walked around the kitchen. One time as she was turning the radio on to a nice country tune she felt a very strong slap on her left shoulder. She turned around and there was no one in the room or even in the house. She believes it was the ghost telling her it didn't like country western music.

The chief ghostly feature of this haunted house seems to be a ghost who like to mess up preparations for meals. "It's like the ghost wants to be part of the family. Incidentally, at meals the children would sometimes set a place for their favorite spook, which seems farfetched, but it does calm the ghostly activities for the night," Bonnie said. "We have seen other mysterious happenings—furniture turned around, chairs and living room end tables moved across the room, salt all over the counters and floor and china flying through the air at the slightest provocation. These odd disturbances consisted largely of poltergeist events and are fairly common in this town," Bonnie concluded.

Now that the little haunted house on South Street has been torn down and only a pile of badly decayed shingles and boards remain on the land, is the place still haunted? Bonnie says, "Why not? For years ghosts have haunted the area, roamed the grounds and become especially active on Halloween. I believe nothing will ever change, and I certainly hope not. We liked our friendly ghosts a lot!"

The Shadow

Michele sent this letter shortly after her father's death:
How is your mom doing?

Tell her for me that I was washing dishes and I saw a shadow go by my head on the right and it startled me. A second after that I felt a very strong presence behind me, the kind you feel when someone is sneaking up behind you, only more intense. I jumped, it startled me so. I stopped with the dishes and looked at the phone. I wanted to call Mom because I felt something had happened to Dad but I stopped because I thought they would think I was nuts. I went to Dan and told him what happened. That was at 6:30 p.m. I got a call a little later and they said my dad had died! He came and said good-bye to me and to tell me everything between us was all right.

I know your mom might appreciate this.

Love,
Michele

Christine's Haunt

A local historian says this area has seen much violence, especially during the Revolutionary War years and during the building of the Erie Canal, which is typical of places that seem inhabited by restless spirits.

"I knew the house had some kind of a spiritual entity within it and it wasn't a very comfortable feeling," Christine told the small group of relatives gathered at her place to help with the renovations. "As soon as we started the work, ghostly activities seemed

74

to step up."

"At first the experiences always happened at night time. It's the weirdest thing. I'd close my eyes and try to concentrate on something besides this strange house, but suddenly I began to hear, like in my mind, my name being called. I'd hear it even with my hands covering my ears. Soon I began to yell out, 'No, don't bother me.' I would be very terrified and sometimes had to leave the house for hours at a time. Of course my husband thought it was all my imagination and refused to believe our house was haunted. That is until he had a few exciting close calls with the spirit.

"On another night, I couldn't get some of the lights to work. When my husband checked them out, everything seemed in place. It was always lights going out, kitchen appliances not working—a lot of electrical manifestations. This ghost kept us and our local electrician busy just trying to keep the house lights and power on. I figured the 'ghost of a dead electrician' must be at fault but my husband thinks it's this 'bad deal' of a house we bought."

Within a few days after they had moved into their home, more eerie incidents ensued. It just happened that there were the right conditions for an apparition. The moon was full, dark clouds eerie incidents began to intrude into their lives. It just happened that there were the right conditions for an apparition. The moon was full, dark clouds skudded across the gray skies from time to time, and the wind blew at the shutters banging them half off their hinges.

"I lay awake tossing and turning through the long dark night," Christine's husband related. "Sometime in the hours before dawn, my unrest grew. My wife was asleep beside me. I tried to sleep but something forced me to keep opening my eyes, and then suddenly I saw a man standing at the foot of my bed, staring at me. I saw him quite distinctly, a tall man in a nondescript dark coat. He was in his late forties with long, black hair and his clothes were from the '20s or '30s. I didn't get time to say a word or to wake up my wife, because the apparition was gone."

"This incident spooked us into taking action," Christine said. "We brought the dogs into our bedroom to sleep with us—either to make us feel safer or in hopes they would scare the intruder. The hall light stayed on until the ghost shut it off and we prayed a lot." But it didn't help; twice in the night, she felt like someone was poking her on the upper arm. Each time she called out to her husband who was asleep and woke him up to investigate but nothing was ever found to account for these nightly disturbances.

Continuing, Christine said, "We have had some real interesting nights! My husband would see a ghostly figure in one room and I would see another about the same time in the opposite end of the house. My ghost was like a mist beside me, pulling at my arm. Our manifestations seem to take place around the clock now, and we are thinking of seeking help soon. We need to get back to a normal life.

"Recently the ghost messed with our stereo. All of a sudden, early in the morning around two-thirty, the stereo started blasting. Then this summer our pipes would bang in the basement when no heat was on. Something, I mean a 'strange something,' is always happening to puzzle us. Perhaps a psychic or more holy water is needed. Until then we will have to live with out ghosts who are a little scary, but nothing overly hostile—so far!"

Library Haunt

"We had just shut the bedroom door when we heard someone shuffling outside in the hall and a knock, knock on the door," the Colonel said.

What surprised him was that he hadn't seen anybody entering the room, nor had heard anyone leaving, nor any voices. After a while he went out into the hall and downstairs. No one in sight.

His son and family were visiting with them for the holidays. Helen, the Colonel's wife, at first thought the grandchildren had been involved in a certain amount of hooliganism but when she checked with them the following morning, found that all were in bed asleep before midnight. The noise and knockings began shortly after that hour. The young boys said they heard the footsteps, but no one had knocked on their door. The footsteps were heard all night long.

The Colonel said the old Ithaca house is supposedly haunted and they have had many such eerie incidents.

"One night in early spring, I was down in the library reading. All of a sudden I caught something out of the corner of my eye and I stood up and looked around and there was a lovely woman standing by my leather chair. It was then that I was hit with an electrical shock. I said, 'Hello, I didn't know we had a guest,' and she started fading!

"This happened only once and I am certain that the woman was no physical being. She walked right through the chair I was sitting in!"

Terry

Some months ago, Terry's story came to my attention. She knew about my research and writings about ghosts. And as soon as Marie and I had finished our dessert, she approached our table with the bill and remarked, "I have read your book of ghosts in Port Byron and liked it very much, but I have a story or two that can top any story in that book!" Then she left us to gather up our packages and coats.

I immediately arranged an interview with her for the following morning at Wells Fargo Diner, where she works as a waitress. "Come early before the customers start arriving," she suggested.

Poogie came along with me to catch all the story just in case I missed a point or two. Besides, she is a "ghost buster" in disguise and has helped me on numerous occasions, especially in haunted houses.

Terry was visibly shaken and apprehensive about telling her story, but after a cup of strong diner coffee, she opened up.

"First of all, let me tell you that I don't consider myself to be psychic or have any talents that would let me contact the dead or anything like that. I lived with the experience for a long time

77

without telling anyone, for fear of ridicule."

It seems that other family members too, had similar eerie happenings. They all believed the apparition in the house was benevolent and was probably their younger sister, Jenny, who died unexpectedly when she was a very young child.

I was frightened when Terry told about her demon infestation. So I encouraged her to give me some history, first of the family home and accounts of the little girl spirit living with them.

The house is situated on Slayton Road about a mile from the town of Conquest, near Pinesville and Pepper Mill. Conquest is a colorful village with a population of about seven hundred. Its residents have been there for many generations, dating back to the Revolutionary War.

Terry's family's house is a lovely white two-story dwelling with a large front porch, spacious lawn and is surrounded with tall pine trees. This house was once a stagecoach inn where travelers were put up for a night, meals were served and some say it was also a boarding house after the stagecoach era. When Terry's dad bought the place from them, all they had to do was "move in"—ghost and all awaited them. Her parents did some remodeling but the main house stayed much the same. The stairway was the original . . . but reinforced so it no longer creaked and the railings were made stronger, but the interior was never changed in any way.

While seated at the vanity in her bedroom she felt a presence close by. "I could feel something coldish behind me," she recalled. "It's hard to explain. I went out of the bedroom to check a possible draft coming from another room. Nothing."

Later that night, she heard a little girl's voice crying. Terry knew it was her dead sister's spirit. She thinks that the large upstairs bedroom seems to be where all the footsteps are heard nightly from 11:30 p.m. until dawn. The footsteps are light, more of a child's stepping. "When an adult walks up the stairs, the floor boards never creak because of the remodeling job on them, but at night each step makes a noise as the tiny ghost walks up them to the bedroom above the dining room."

Once it "la-la-la'd" a song to her. Terry was fifteen years old at the time. It sang throughout the summer, always the same tune, but only for one summer and only between 10 and 10:30 p.m.

One summer day Terry, who was babysitting all the young ones, saw her dead sister's spirit near the clothesline; she thought she would faint. She was hanging the wet clothes, all the time wondering where the rest of the kids were, when suddenly the spirit appeared; blond curls, wearing a party dress and smiling. Then she disappeared.

The spirit of her little sister, Jenny, seems to be house-bound and loving to family members. They all have seen her at one time or another and no one seems disturbed but welcome her presence. She was a year younger than Terry when she died of burns when their house caught fire. Jenny's spirit is with her daily and always at Christmas time when she appears by the Christmas tree for a brief second.

Terry stopped her storytelling, swallowed hard and wet her lips. This next episode with Jenny always makes her eyes fill with tears and her voice breaks from time to time. She loved her sister very much, one can easily hear this as she talks about their short time together.

Jenny had died in 1965. Before her death she had given Terry a locket and Terry's husband seems to think that her ghost needs to be near the locket and Terry . . . both were special in her short life. Jenny's spirit often moves glasses about and someone is always taking Terry's personal things and leaving them downstairs, behind or in dressers. Once when Terry was in bed and had her light on, she warned her family that she wanted the light on throughout the night, and held the string in her hand to make sure no one shut it off. She was fifteen at the time. Then around the time the footsteps are always heard, something touched her shoulder. Terry was awake and alone. She saw nothing, but the light went out. She didn't sleep alone that night or ever again!

The little ghosts' footsteps are always heard in the big bedroom circling around and around.

This next incident brought shivers to us all as Terry continued her ghostly encounters with Jenny's spirit. When Terry was moving out of this house to her own home, she had gone upstairs to get her things. She had the feeling that someone didn't want her to leave; Jenny called out her name, "Terry, Terry," She ran downstairs and told her mom who flew up to the room to check this out.

Her mom saw nothing, that is until her husband died. She would never admit to the house being haunted but soon after her husband's funeral, things began to frighten her, especially since she had moved upstairs. Noises still wake her in the middle of the night, clocks stop working; one ghost was seen walking through one of the big wall clocks and immediately it stopped.

Terry said that whenever she smells roses she knows her dad is around. He loved his rose garden and was always picking them for their kitchen table.

And Jenny's spirit continues to hang around to warn the family at the time of a family crisis. Her little voice was heard the night before disaster hit them. Family members claim to hear the little girl's voice humming an old tune. Whenever Jenny was worried about something, she hummed this song.

Terry laughed tearfully and explained that she has had a conversation with the little ghost. "Please be a good ghost," Terry whispered. And so they continue a life together, the two of them. Terry said, "Even now Jenny and I have an occasional meeting!"

Old Stoneface

I hate typing this story . . . believe me. I have heard of a writer who refused to finish a piece on a ghost story because so many strange things began happening to him. Well, I have been working on this demonic tale for several months now and to this day, I dislike discussing or writing up this eerie case. Then there is the old literary proverb, "Never write and fear no one!" Or something like that.

You will see that with this story of Terry and the Conquest demon, we have reached the edge of the region of ghostly tales.

These are actual, terrifying accounts that you will want to read with the lights on in every room.

This particular demon story illustrates that a haunting can last many years. In Terry's case of phenomenal happenings and scary events, they have been taking place over more than twenty years, involving many family members.

Terry started to doubt her own sanity, the infestation had gotten so bad. The children were beginning to be hurt and scared constantly, day and night. She and her mom found out soon enough that reality couldn't explain what was going on in their home.

"I'm used to disbelief and all sorts of insults about my ghostly encounters, but I believe that when you brush up against evidence of the demonic, the dark forces want to warn you away."

Terry is pretty and a very sensible woman; very loving, and that's what made her experiences all the more horrifying. The entire family all are deeply disturbed by it all.

Unhappily for Terry and the family, the gradual disappearance of her younger sister's spirit was accompanied by the coming of another, more menacing figure . . . Old Stoneface, as the family came to call this horrible ghostly figure.

As Terry gazed about, she was astonished to see Old Stoneface at the window. Eager to have a closer look, she stepped forward, but as she did, the demon vanished as suddenly as it had appeared. That single experience was incredible enough, but when Terry returned to the same spot the following night, the vision reappeared exactly as it had before, and vanished once again. Equally incredible, her brothers and sister saw the same vision just as clearly.

Wednesday, the same day of the week but several weeks later, Terry heard a noise against the house. It was a dark, starless night and she was babysitting the young ones. They asked, "What was that?" "The ivy blowing against the window," she answered in her frightened voice. But it wasn't the ivy. It was someone tapping at the window. On the outer side of the window, clinging to the sash was Old Stoneface!

Terry stared after him with narrowed eyes. She had not exaggerated; he was ugly and scary with a peculiar flat face and large terrible eyes as red as fire. He frowned angrily at her, then leaped away pulling open the sash and fled down the rolling hill without looking back. "I can only tell you that I had never in all my life seen anything more terrifying than that face," Terry said. "I remember screaming for help but I could barely hear the sound of my own voice above the noise of the growling, inhuman Stoneface. There seemed to be a gale blowing all the time the apparition was standing there," she told us.

The apparition described as a hunchbacked, horned-headed figure in black clothing made its appearances regularly throughout the summer months. Notable for its two-horned head, this fearsome ghost often appeared when Terry and her brothers were at the kitchen table playing games. It seemed bent on distracting them.

Once, Terry recalled the demon deliberately raised its head at the window after it had supposedly vanished. His image is always seen through the same window.

He, Old Stoneface, seems to like children. He always appears to them and either growls or strolls by them as they play between the homes on that road. This demon is not a spirit. Terry thinks at some time in the past it was brought there by someone with strong powers such as the Witch of Spook Woods. Once Laura, her younger sister, saw the demon while she was alone in the kitchen. And Terry's son was terrified when he witnessed its raging fit and growling noises in the back field.

For several months, according to Terry, the night appearances continued. They saw Stoneface as many as two dozen times, and four years ago they brought the demon into the house by a seance . . . the four younger children, David, Mindy, Shelly and Laura were toying with the spirit, trying to call it when suddenly it came through the window, growled, circled them and then went out the back window. It sounded like broken glass falling to the floor as it left. Upon investigating, there was no broken glass and the windows were still locked; the house looked untouched.

Terry said that one night chaos erupted in the dark hall upstairs. Her brother and sister threw themselves against the bedroom door, intent in keeping out Old Stoneface. The others knelt outside by the door, praying and fighting some tangible force of

82

evil. They all suffered emotionally from the malevolent force that attacked their home. The rest of the night passed peacefully, but the moment with Stoneface was etched forever in their minds.

Even after these nights of terror, her family chose to remain in their haunted house. But in desperation, Terry called a psychic from Syracuse for help. It was a decision made by the entire family after another sighting of Old Stoneface's horrible body staring at them through the same old window. "Do you have the faintest idea of the terror inflicted not just momentarily, but lastingly, on us. How we survived the shock, we'll never understand."

The psychic's credentials included tours to many haunted houses in the state. He remarked that Central New York is a breeding ground for ghosts and he told Terry he had seen similar episodes in other haunted houses. After assuring her and her family that they would no longer be bothered, he collected a tidy fee and left. But the hauntings continued.

The next thing Terry tried was an exorcist from upstate. He was a very strong and courageous man. The ceremony was for a time successful, but little by little the house became infested again. This was especially tough on the small children. The growling sounds and the tappings on the window were back and the odor of the demon was everywhere.

Then the following evening the psychic came to the house again. It was raining and the lightning flashed continuously as they sat in the living room. Suddenly he said to them, "There's an evil spirit in this room, I sensed it as I walked toward the window. The entity came from the hall doorway." He told them they should keep the shades down and put saucers of vinegar around; ghosts stay away from vinegar.

Nothing has worked for Terry . . . ghosts still haunt the place.

Merry and the Poltergeist

Merry seems to think a poltergeist lives in her house or lived there when they were all young. They played games with "it"!

One evening when their father was at work and their mom was out milking the cow (and they should have been in bed . . . past 10 o'clock by the old wall clock), they decided to sneak down to the kitchen for a snack. As they sat at the table having milk and cookies, they saw a fishing reel roll out of the bedroom and across the kitchen floor. They weren't afraid, just their friendly ghost and they knew exactly what to do . . . they rolled the reel back into the bedroom. A few seconds later it rolled out again and they giggled and knew their ghost was playing with them again. It had often happened in the past. Again they rolled it back into the room; no sooner than it had disappeared into the bedroom, it came flying out the doorway and hit the wall behind them.

Now they realized their little game with the ghost was getting a bit out of control and decided it was time to stop. They were scared and rushed back to bed.

They never told their parents—it would have been spanking time for all.

The White Dove of Seneca Falls

A remarkable haunting took place in the early 1920s in this delightful Finger Lakes town which was mourning the sudden death of a young boy. A white dove appeared and flew for three days and nights around the young dead boy's home.

Neighbors calling at the home to pay their respects heard a peculiar sound which seemed to emanate from the floor under the coffin. One saw the great white dove perched on the boy's coffin. They chased it outside but it always managed to return mysteriously and stay near the boy's body. As family members thrust out their hands to seize it, the dove vanished. Shortly after it was perched on the coffin again and remained there until the day of the funeral.

That was a very sad day for all. The weary white dove followed the funeral procession to the gravesite and remained atop a tall pine tree until dusk.

Local parishioiners thought the spectral bird was the restless spirit of the youth who dies before his time.

Almond's Headstone

One hot summer afternoon, two young boys, ages ten and eleven, were playing in the Pine Hill Cemetery, across the road from their aunt's home.

They were having a fun time . . . reading old headstone inscriptions and playing hide-n-seek, resting from time to time beneath the shade of the tall monuments. Most of their conversation was about who could find the oldest headstone.

It was around one p.m. when they found the Almond grave site. It had an old iron gate, rusted off its hinges, swinging from its iron fence post. Inside the square cemetery plot, headstones lined up in a row marked the descendents, dating as far back as 1700.

Matt, the younger boy, noticed a small headstone toppled over and tried to turn it upright, but it was too heavy so he called to Mike for help. The two of them tried to fix the old stone but it would not budge. It looked as if it had lain there unattended for years. There was grass and moss covering the sides and top of it. The front of the stone was sunken into the ground and almost completely covered with sod. They wanted to know who was buried there. The smaller stone seemed to indicate a child's grave.

After several hours of play and stone reading, they decided to go back to the Almond plot again and see if they could fix that fallen headstone. For some unknown reason it bothered them to see it so badly neglected.

They were horror-stricken . . . the Almond headstone was upright. Some dirt still covered the inscription but it was standing alongside the others in the fenced-in plot.

The two were so frightened that they ran back to their house as fast as their legs would carry them. But no one was there, so they screamed and ran to the neighbor's house. Old Ed, the town assessor, lived there . . . another short distance from Pine Hill.

He told the boys they must be wrong because visitors have tried for years to lift that stone but it wouldn't move an inch. Even grave maintenance men had never been able to straighten it . . . "much too heavy," he said in his low, authoritative voice. "If you look at it on a full moon night, the headstone glows with a silvery brightness. None of the others shine, only little Almond's."

A single moonstone in the cemetery scares the travelers passing by, but they know it is harmless . . . the child was only five when he died. His father's wagon overturned at the bridge and the young Almond boy drowned.

Matt kept remembering an inscription on the largest monument in the cemetery:

Here waits
John Matthew
Who touches this stone
Shall live no longer
Than his shadow

The Almond moss-covered headstone still rests deeply in the sod—on its side. Again.

Second-Hand Shop

Al has a second-hand shop built on the site of the old Eagle Hotel. It was probably from past owners that the wildest popular whispers and rumors derived. Such as: "Never pick up an old comb. It is considered bad luck for fear of the restless soul of its former owner."

Big Al and the other local antique dealers, King's Settlement, Yesterdays, Memory Lane and the Old Erie, who operate businesses on Main Street, say they have been told by reputable merchants that souls of the women who owned these personal articles still inhabit them. It is believed that the air of the supernatural clings to combs especially. Like other articles of intimate and long use, such as clothing and mirrors traditionally associated with ladies, combs are believed to take on something of the soul of the one who owned it. One woman, probably a white witch the dealer said, advised that when she feels a comb is too heavy with sadness, she purifies it by several washes and soakings in rainwater.

Most antique dealers boast of weird incidents happening from time to time in their shops. Big Al says his ghost is an eccentric permanent ghost-guest. In the dark silent night, he paces the upstairs rooms. The distant sounds of footsteps, and the clashing of glasses, echo out of the walls astounding the family and at times his customers. Al had initially been reluctant to report the ghostly noises but was encouraged when he heard of many similar haunted places around him.

All sorts of spooking incidents have happened to him. He has gone into his storerooms to find books and other objects moved from boxes to shelves and vice versa. He says the lights go off and on and footsteps are heard walking into the upstairs bedrooms. When he investigates the noises and turns on the light and there is nothing but an empty room, he turns off the light and then the footsteps begin again. It just keeps going on and on. "I tried this little spooky game all one night, but the ghost won; I fell asleep before dawn on the bedroom floor."

Another manifestation at the shop was a recurring smell of lilacs, almost suffocating at times. People would be looking around for lilac bushes as they shopped.

The latest eerie incident has one of our local antique dealers puzzled. As he tells it:

"A very large oriental curio cabinet, recently purchased from a house sale, had been temporarily deposited on the staircase landing between the second and third floors. This piece of furniture was heavy; it took two burly movers to get it up the stairs." Around midnight, the antique dealer had gone up to the third floor to check out a banging noise and the furniture was on the landing; when he came back down the oriental piece was not there. It was on the floor at the bottom of the staircase! And he was alone in his shop at the time!

Whenever he hears dishes and pots and pans banging about, Al shrugs his shoulders and remembers this old home has had some very interesting tenants. Mr. Wethey, a funeral director, lived here and had his caskets on display in the front living room facing the street. In the back of the house, the "casket warehouse" was often the scene of some rather frightening happenings. Neighbors were afraid to walk past the building after dark. Its proximity to the cemetery didn't help. They believed that corpses floated about after midnight between the two deserted haunts.

Despite all this talk, Big Al says this is a very friendly house. The ghosts are here and they aren't doing anything to hurt us and aren't even particularly scary. His theory about the ghosts is that they might be women, who had lived in this stately home because of the smell of lilacs, and other perfumes and the dainty footstep noises.

Antique Ghosts

Mike, from King's Settlement Antiques, lives in the Rabourn House. Lights turn on and off, noises come from the walls late at night and there are so many scary incidents happening that most of the other tenants won't step one foot into his part of the old haunted house even though he has yet to see any real ghosts

At Memory Lane, the owner said that the only ghost manifestation is perhaps the antique clothing stored upstairs that always seems to be messed up, or thrown about on the floor and never in the place they set up for their display. Is there a ghostly shopper looking for an old outfit?

According to local legend, in winter, usually about Christmas time when the snow covers Main Street, the marks of horses' hooves have been seen on the frozen snow at the spot where the Eagle Hotel hitching post once stood. Perhaps it's a Season's Greeting from the founder of this unique canal town!

Ouija Board Message

Becca had a ouija board in her closet and it was never used with much success . . . that is until the night she and several of her school friends decided to have some fun with it.

Earlier in the week they had been across the road in the Pine Hill Cemetery looking at graves and, to their surprise, they found several graves with the same last name and same date of death.

They immediately drove back to Becca's college to investigate the deaths in the college's "autopsy and deaths" records department. They found that the father killed the entire family and himself. What a frightening day that was but they still wanted more spookiness. That is when they decided to invite the gang over for a ouija board party.

That particular ouija board has caused two of Becca's friends some terrifying moments. Mike, who knew the cemetery murder story, recalled that he and his friend, Chris, had a ouija board scare as recently as the week before. Chris, who was new to the area, had never heard the story, so the two boys walked to the grave sites with the ouija board. Mike, who was afraid of nothing, was eager to go "spirit hunting." They sat on the graves and asked for a spirit. Nothing. They asked again if the murdered family had a spirit here. Nothing. After awhile they laid the ouija board down on a headstone and began to talk about sports and less scary subjects when suddenly the "eye" of the board moved to "yes" with no one touching it!

Forgetting the board and their hats, they ran out of the cemetery as fast as their legs would carry them.

After this story, Becca said, they put the board on the living room floor and sat around it. They started to ask questions to bring a spirit into the room. They kept working with the ouija board for several minutes but nothing was happening.

Sue and Sean went first. When they put their fingers on the board, the "thing" that moves around suddenly went to the letter "S." Then one of the boys suggested they ask the board for more letters. Now they were all a little nervous. The board was working. The board definitely had a message for them. The "thing" moved to "S" again and again . . . and they kept asking for more letters. Then it happened . . . it spelled out S A M; they asked "Sam who?" No one could come up with a Sam they knew of. Becca touched the little thing that moves around, as she calls it, and her fingers got about two inches from it and it went right off the board. And it happened every time someone other than Sue and Sean tried to touch it.

After a few minutes, Mike from Montezuma said he knew of a Sam who died a few years ago. Then Mike asked the board, "Are you Sam Johnson?" The eye of the board moved to "yes," but they weren't convinced and needed more letters. "Where do you live?" The "planchette" or "thing" moved around quickly to the letter "T," then r, then e, e, s . . . TREES they all shouted. But what about trees, Mike asked the board. Nothing. The thing moved to the letter "S" again. Now, they were very uptight. The board was not only working and spelling, but it was in a hurry. Sue and Sean's hands were being guided but with much more speed than they could handle.

Mike, who was now asking the questions, sat nowhere near the board. He told Becca and friends that when he was a young kid, he knew of a Sam whose father grew Christmas trees . . . that was it. It was Sam and the nursery trees. They all began to relax . . . all but Becca who knew nothing of a Sam and wanted more from this spirit. She asked, "How do we know it's you?" It spelled out T R E E S. Still unsure, she asked the time. Sue and Sean had no watch on and there was no clock in the living room. The board replied 12:37 a.m. Two of the kids ran out to check the kitchen clock . . . 12:37 a.m.!

No one had any idea of the time because they'd been in the living room for hours talking and laughing and calling spirits.

At this point they all were scared and began to feel this was no game for amateurs. One of the girls who was seated near the board knew more about ouija boards and she said she could sense a great deal of negativity and that she was leaving for home. She warned them to stay away from the board, that it was dangerous and that she would be over the next day.

90

Becca said that the rest of the night, they hid under blankets and beds waiting for dawn to brighten up the place.

The next day Becca babysat for her new neighbor, and told her about the "Sam" incident. Becca knew nothing about this family except that they had built a new home next to hers and had two little girls.

Becca was shocked to learn from the mother that she had a brother Sam who died in a gun accident. They all believe Sam came to tell them he was still around . . . just one door down from his sister's house—having a party. A Ouija Party!

Kate's Ghostly Encounters

Kate is a very interesting and rather high-powered young lady. At the time of her story she was a student at college and working part-time.

She often came home late and would start cooking meals for her roommate and for Shawn, the landlady-actress's daughter. Kate said she always felt that someone was leaning over her shoulder when she was working in the kitchen. Once she asked a date to fix a sandwich for her. He came running out of the kitchen saying he was sure someone was in there with him but he couldn't see them. He made the sandwich in Kate's room.

Shawn's room had a lot of eerie things going on. Once Kate thought she heard books falling off the shelves. She opened the door but all the books were still on the shelves. Shawn's room was young Zachery's room before his death.

Another spooky incident happened whenever Kate would put the key into the apartment door. She could hear the voices of a young person and an older woman. Probably Zachery and his mom talking, they all believed.

Once Diane, the landlady, put a bag of hats in the hallway and went off to do an errand and when she came back, each room had one hat in it. No one was at home except Diane at the time.

One thing that rather upset Kate was a picture of a cat hanging on the wall . . . the picture would swing back and forth, the cat in the picture moved as well.

When Kate decided to paint her room she invited some friends over to help, but after a few hours of hauntings, they wouldn't go out of her room to get anything . . . not even a glass of water from the kitchen.

Three roommates came up from her college to spend the weekend with her, but they all were scared of the place and left after a few hours, believing in ghosts.

One young actress who stayed with Kate was so very frightened she refused to walk in the hallway alone; she felt as if someone was walking close behind her. At the end of the hallway was a large mirror and the young girl looked into it and saw a shadowy figure trying to get away or move from side to side in front of the mirror, as if it had been cornered by her. The shadow eventually found a way out and disappeared. This girl went back to Los Angeles a full believer!

When Kate was looking out the window, she heard her name being called out from within the house. This happened every time she looked out the window. She knew there was some kind of spirit standing behind her and it always made her feel a little uncomfortable.

The door had bells that rang when someone was about to enter. Well, they would ring at all hours of the day and night and no one was near them.

Shawn said that she couldn't believe her eyes when the lighted candle at the end of her room moved in mid-air across to the farthest end and fell to the floor.

Incidents multiplied. Some things became so usual that Kate just took them for granted. Once she was entertaining some friends and when she went into the kitchen for more refreshments, she could hear her name called out from Zach's room. That really spooked everyone.

Kate tells of having trouble with her phone cord jumping up and down rhythmically in two to three second intervals. There is no apparent explanation for this. She was alone in the house. No pets. Not even a breeze from anywhere. She just stood there with her hands shaking. To this very day, she wonders a little if her phone cord will start jumping around again.

Shortly after this last incident, Kate had her first glimpse of one of the entities that might have been causing the hauntings. She was going up the stairs late at night, and there on the landing was a tall, slender man wearing outdated clothes. She just kept walking and suddenly he wasn't there. According to Kate, several other tenants saw this same ghostly figure and so did at least two of her friends.

Is the place still haunted? Kate moved back home a few years ago, but she says she thinks it is, but the new tenants aren't talking about it!

Indian Spirits

I was having a manicure at the spa when the manicurist started a conversation about the stars, astrology, moon-phases and their effect on our lives. Well, she came from California and was in her early twenties, and I understood her love for all that star-talk and belief. But when we discovered we had the same last name, instantly we became friends and she then began to slowly unfold the many trials and tribulations of her interesting and sometimes unbelievable life. Her "brush" with the spirits did get my undivided attention and I prayed for a strong surge of memory cells to take over . . . with both hands soaking in skin softener, there was no way I could write down any notes.

At first I did not want to ask too many questions and I didn't mention I collected ghost stores for fear she would clam up; instead I remained silent and let her ramble on about the spirited world she often entered.

Lisa was whispering now because she didn't want the other spa employees to hear her. They didn't believe her stories and acted strangely towards her after her first encounter with a "spirit." Now she refrains from telling them anything personal.

Lisa is unmarried . . her only companion is her cat who sleeps with her every night.

Three weeks ago she was in bed alone—her cat refused to sleep with her preferring to hide in the closet. On this particular night the stars were in line with Jupiter and brighter than usual; a spirit realm surrounded her body giving her the feeling of power and strength.

Lying there, she suddenly realized that there was someone in the room with her. She didn't know where to look first; checking the doorway, she saw nothing but a smoky film drifting about. The windows were open . . . that could be the reason for the eerie smoke.

Terror-stricken, she realized someone was sitting at the bottom of the bed; the mattress was squashed down, she explained. At first she closed her eyes, then opened them and saw the ghostly figure of an old Indian! He didn't look at her but stared straight ahead at the bedroom wall. She said that he really wasn't ghost-like, his body had substance.

Around his neck he wore a magic string of beads, powerful against acts of malevolent nature, she said. If there was a storm in the lake, he would escape it by dropping one bead from his neck-lace. If the thunder rolled, he needed only to hang the beads on a tree limb, and most important, he could use them to frighten away all the Chepi (ghosts). Incredible tales are told of his bravery and his magic power, Lisa whispered.

"The Indian spirit never moved or made any sound . . . just seemed to be resting on the bed and staring into space! The spirit-image lasted several seconds . . . too long for me, and just as I was about to jump out of bed, the old Indian vanished. I am not afraid of spirits and I believe we all have a guardian spirit, but an Indian spirit sitting at the bottom of my bed did mess up my mind!"

In her half-dreaming state, Lisa had forgotten the Indian Chief of Superstition Mountain—a picturesque Indian who lived to a great age and who was much admired and trusted by his people.

It was as simple as that. She had seen the ethereal vision of the Indian Chief of Superstition Mountain, dressed in full ceremonial clothes.

"I feel odd just sitting here talking to you," she continued. "I

94

have told this story to a few of my fellow workers here and they think I am crazy. So please, don't mention it to the hairdresser when you leave my booth to get your hair washed. Most of them laugh it off and think I have been studying the stars and fortune cards, but 'What's there, is there.' "

Lisa had some intriguing historical touches to add before finishing her ghost story. She said, "My apartment building is built on an Indian burial ground, and many Indian artifacts came from this spot.

The Wind Ghost

Ghostly incidents are happening all the time; a recent event occurred on a sunny afternoon in late August at a unique bookstore in Central New York. This building is very old, constructed sometime during the early 1800s. The land around the structure and directly beneath was once part of a tract of land occupied by the Cayuga Indians, some say it was their burial grounds; others say it was just Indian land.

The proprietor is Connie, a very active historical researcher and author of many magazine articles and book reviews. She spends many long hours in her bookstore searching for history material to be used in our schools. Little did she know what was to follow as she worked night after night in her little library.

Connie has never seen a spine-chiller ghost, but there have been some very strange things happening, particularly in the back section where the great novels and Shakespearean plays are neatly stacked.

It was while she was walking along the aisle of these old books that she first saw the "wind ghost" apparition. The figure disappeared immediately. As it passed, she felt an exceedingly cold gust of air pass by her cheek. The phenomenon has repeated itself many times. Connie cautiously told her husband about her experiences and as she might have expected, he rejected her story and dismissed it as a product of an overactive imagination.

She said the best time to see ghosts or feel their presence is late at night or on Sunday when there are few people about. Things are more likely to be noticeable at those times; also, some psychics mentioned to her that spirits tend to shy away from the vibrations of large groups.

There are two major unexplained events Connie reported that occurred during the after-closing hours.

"I heard a plaintive sigh in the corner area once, as if someone was standing near me, but there was nobody there. Another time I heard the sound of feet in the upstairs floors where our living quarters are, but again no one was up there."

Who or what haunts this bookstore? It has been speculated by some researchers that the physical disturbances of the structure may well release the psychic information that is "stored" within it. There are some vague notions buried deep in the lore of the building, that the spirit of a woman does indeed linger there. And Connie has a few stories to prove it. "I believe in ghosts but I am not afraid of them," she remarked before beginning another eerie tale. Then she smiled sheepishly at me and whispered (because there were a few customers milling around the store), "You know, I met the loveliest, yet strangest woman recently. She came into the store late one afternoon. My eyes caught her as soon as she entered. She was nice looking, somewhere near forty years old and was very well-dressed.

"As I watched, the lady took a deep breath and looked around. She then slowly turned her head and gazed away into space. It was as if something in the store had gotten her attention.

"Later, as I was handing her change and the book she had purchased, she looked at me very seriously and asked, 'Has anyone ever told you there are spirits in this store?'

"No, but if the 'book spirit' is here, I don't mind at all," Connie laughed. The lady blinked her big brown eyes and looked very abruptly at her. Then she asked, "Have any of the books ever acted oddly?" Connie knew of a few incidents but she has never told any customers about them. She felt it was none of their concern and besides it might scare some of them away.

She had watched as books mysteriously fell from securely-stacked shelves. Late one evening, she had gazed incredulously as one book seemed to work its way out of a line and gently float to the nearby reading table. Then another, and another, fluttering in the air as if forcefully pried out by ghostly fingers. She has tried in vain to explain this; the wind could cause it, but she reasoned there was simply no wind, no breeze, no gust of air of any kind capable of pushing books out of the shelves so selectively and so powerfully. There was no logical explanation.

The strange lady stepped toward the front door and concluded by saying that the bookstore is haunted but that the spirit that haunts it is very kind. Connie switched off the lights as she followed a few yards behind her.

She saw the figure in her light cream-colored dress and white floppy hat disappear for a few seconds, then appear between two tall book racks and start to pull first one book, then another from the shelves. The lady seemed to want to find something and not necessarily a book!

A week later the she was back again. This time she asked Connie if she remembered her. "I was wearing a broad-brimmed hat." Connie smiled and answered, "Yes." Then the lady continued, "You know your store has a ghost in it again today." Connie softly answered that she wasn't a bit surprised because she has always felt that she was never alone there.

The lovely lady stepped closer to the counter and told her that when she was there last, she felt something breeze through her hair as she was standing near the novels shelf. She then took her hat off and the ghost floated around her head and gently lifted her hair off her neck. It had kind of a wind body.

Before the strange lady left, Connie gave her a book on travels and hoped she would enjoy reading it.

Yesterday, Connie received a thank you note from the lovely lady. The writing was so different from anything she had ever seen before, that she had difficulty making out the words. It was very short and signed "Jean." No last name and no return address!

In all likelihood, there are still "book spirits" inside this bookstore. Stop by sometime. Browse through the books and magazines but beware if you feel that unnerving sensation that someone if looking over your shoulder or a cool breeze lifts your hair off your neck. Have a look . . . it might be the "wind ghost."

Could it be that this store is still haunted?

Behm Story

The summers were short and unpredictable.
The winters long and dark and snowy.
The haunts were everywhere!

—Behm

As he was driving home from his job at the sugar beet plant, he came onto the Conquest Road around midnight when he saw an old woman standing near the middle of the road. Her flowing gray hair covered most of her facial features. As she trundled down the white line toward his truck, she seemed to be floating a few inches above the road.

"There was a bright light surrounding her," he said, "and I was blinking from the silvery haze in front of me. When I could see clearly, there was an ugly old woman on the hood of the truck. Her face was close to the windshield, her purple colored mouth slightly closed. She was scowling and screwing up her small, beady eyes to see in, shading them with one hand.

"Then her eyes lifted slowly, focused into mine. They opened wide and I thought I was going to wreck my truck I was so scared. We stared at each other through the glass and then I saw her leap in front of the truck.

"I drove through her!"

They found him staring at the empty road a short distance down from the frightful spot. The neighbors ran back and found nothing. He drove back to the scene, prepared to see the old woman again, but the air was empty. The road showed no signs of any accident. The old woman had disappeared leaving no trace that she had ever been there.

It took some moments for the truth to register . . . she was a ghost!

Apple Dryer Haunt

People have seen ghosts since the beginning of time, and there is no reason to think that their reports are made up. They have been seen as floating lights, as life-like people who disappear through walls and forms in cloudy, white, sheets. It doesn't take a dramatic encounter with a ghost to be aware of them.

One woman told me about her grandfather who had seen a ghost who lived in the old apple dryer building located on the corner of Route 31 and King Street.

Every night a candle glowed in the window of the old building. One night it would appear in the front window of the structure, then perhaps in one of the middle rooms, or near the back windows. It was seen for years. But whenever the citizens of the town entered the room where the candlelight was shining, it suddenly went out and there remained total darkness. No one was ever found occupying the rooms.

The candlelight mystery was never solved. The old dryer has long been gone and now the present building is empty. Or is the ghost still in residency there?

Breaker-boy Phantom

When Charlie was a young man, he was a breaker-boy in the gypsum mine near Rochester. Charlie called it a plaster mine.

One afternoon he was working alone in the mine shaft, making his way to the loaded gypsum car, when he felt his coat sleeve being tugged. He turned quickly to see who was pulling at it. No one was there.

It was without a doubt the ghost of old miner Joe, who was a breaker-boy many years ago. No one ever seemed alarmed at his appearances; his spirit was not especially harmful, yet Charlie could feel his whole body quivering with fright. He had heard many tales about dead miners who rise and walk about the tunnels as they had lived, indistinguishable from the living, except he and the others knew the gang and Joe had long since departed this world in the last mine disaster.

A ghostly voice from a distance suddenly yelled out, "Lie down, lie down. Flat on the ground!"

Charlie flung himself frantically onto the sandy white floor and hid his head underneath his arms. He could not estimate the time he lay there—motionless—alone. Although he was frightened and achingly cold, he finally pulled himself to his knees. Blinking, he gazed around and his stomach turned with horror. A dozen lighted candles shone on the track ahead of him. He could see the fallen boulder crushing his mine car and he could see "ghostly Joe" standing beside it.

Quickly he scrambled toward the mine exit, gasping and praying hysterically. Just before he left the mine, he heard the entire tunnel collapsing behind him. Then Joe's voice came again for the last time, through the dusty mine, "Goodbye breaker-boy."

The mine was shut down and the workers were sent home.

As the mine wagon proceeded up the hill toward Sir Laurence's boarding house, Charlie and the gang cried aloud, "We're alive . . . thanks to ghostly Joe."

The "Spirit" of Halloween

Halloween, with its eerie legends, is fast upon us. Ghostly, ghastly events make good tales for the midnight hour. We all know that October is the time for haunted houses to bring forth their ectoplasmic bodies and scare the daylights out of us.

This ghost story may seem incredible to many, but nevertheless I give it my full belief for I know our canal towns have been subject to prodigious events and phenomenons. Indeed, I have heard many stranger stories than this, along these old Erie towns.

This strange tale actually happened around the year 1925 at one of the last saloons still in business along the towpath of the Erie Canal.

Jeppo was having a drink at the bar, as was his custom and where he was well-known, when an old inhabitant of the town mentioned a ghost story of interest to him.

The storyteller began, "You see this canal was built one hundred years ago, to be exact; it was dug by the Irish. With pick and shovel, workers dug out the boulders, fashioned the towpath on one side and the berm on the other. It took seven years, but it got built—all 363 miles of it. New York paid for it—some seven million dollars!

"You probably don't remember, but in the early years the boats were drawn by mules. We liked mules because they weren't prone to jump off the bridges as horses were and, besides, drivers could forecast the weather by the droop of a mule's ears."

The old timer stopped to catch his breath and take a slug of his beer. At this point Jeppo's mind began to wander back to his younger days. He knew the Erie story; his father was a boatman on the *Seneca Chief* when it made its first voyage through the entire length of the grand canal from the port of Buffalo to the port of New York. He especially liked hearing his father tell of the day where the "Yorkers" were running across the fields, "climbing on trees" and "crowding the banks" to gaze upon the welcome sight of boats along the canal.

The old timer lit up a well-chewed cigar but never missed a beat in his conversation. "I remember some rough times on this water. I heard about this mule driver who battled a ghost in the Montezuma marshes—a spirit with a 'demon face and great flashing green eyes.' "

Jeppo knew now that a true canaller could "jure" up one of these spirits day or night. He was also aware that most of the saloon's patrons had their share of ghosts, witches and other such superstitions and spirit-lore, especially the Irish who, according to his father, "buried their pixies into the canal with loving care."

"I'm an Erie boatman and I haven't seen a ghost yet," Jeppo said lifting his beer mug to his mustache-covered lips. Finishing it in one gigantic gulp and turning to the bartender, he mumbled, "and I'm not about to start debating things like spirits at this late hour. Besides it's Halloween night and you fellows should have more respect for the spirits, if they do exist." Jeppo wasn't sure what he believed . . . most of his life he had heard that "all Hallows Eve" as his mother called it, was the night when ghosts are reputed to hold sway and be able to return and be visible. But for many years now all seemed quiet on the "supernatural" front, so there wasn't any reason to worry about it. Jeppo left the bar.

The late October evening was very dark and the road was deserted. Jeppo shuffled along in a happy mood, and whistled an old canal tune as he stepped onto the high-bridge, a structure that spanned the canal not far from the saloon.

He shivered as the stroke of midnight sounded from the church belfry, perhaps "juring" up an image of one of the spirits discussed earlier in the evening. He walked a little faster, very close to the bridge railing. He whistled more softly; he had no time to lose, all sorts of unpleasant ideas began to cross his mind.

Suddenly, a voice from the canal water broke into song, surprising him:

Low bridge, ev'rybody down,
Low bridge, we must be gettin' near a town,
You can always tell your neighbor
You can always tell your pal,
If he's ever navigated on the Erie Canal.

For a moment he was frightened but curiosity overcame his fear; making sure that he was not seen, he crept round the canal shanty and watched the stranger near the stone wall look towards the bridge and then quickly tie up his boat.

Full of beer, Jeppo was a little slow getting around the shanty to the wharl that ran along the side of the canal. Despite the alcohol, he managed to reach the towpath. He took a few short steps up the path and he could now see someone coming toward him. The slow steps stopped. The stranger was standing directly in front of him.

For a moment he simply held his breath and waited. Jeppo wondered what a canaller and his boat were doing on the Erie at this time of the year! The young canaller was taller than Jeppo. His hair was long and his square jaw was dark red with several days' beard. His cheeks were hollow and there was a wildness in his puffy eyes that the shadows concealed.

He spoke with a slight Irish accent, his clothes were well-tailored and his high-top shoes glowed in the foggy darkness. The figure seemed to be illuminated from within. Something else was not quite right. Jeppo glanced at the boat and realized he'd never seen anything quite like it.

Jeppo knew that the packet boats, mule teams, the lusty two-fisted canawlers as he loved to call them, all had vanished years ago. What was going on here?

After a few awkward seconds of silence, he asked the stranger, "Are you from these parts?"

"No, Sir," the canaller answered back in a husky brogue.

With this the stranger stepped closer and began a long-winded conversation with Jeppo, stopping only to check his boat lines. "I remember some sad times back in the early days. Many boatmen were found dead along the waterway especially around the smaller towns. One boatman who was killed by the doublelocks never really knew what hit him, but I know. He was working on a bullhead boat and had to stand on the cabin roof to steer."

Between the top of the cabin and the bridges there was very little clearance; if the steersman didn't see the bridge in time, he was swept off by the bridge timbers. Many a canaller was killed or crippled by this type of boat.

"I knew he didn't commit suicide as many have reported, it was an accidental death. He was backing up, hit his head on the bridge timbers and fell overboard, as I said. One thing that puzzled everyone was why he never ducked when the bridge came up. When you've been on the canal as long as he had, you know where every bridge is and how far you've got to duck.

"That boatman is still out there. It wasn't his time to die and when you go before your time, you never really leave this earth."

Looking back at the bridge, Jeppo said, "It's getting late and I'll be heading for home now." He started to walk away and had taken several steps before realizing that the stranger hadn't answered him. He turned to wave goodbye but the canaller was gone and so was the boat! They had vanished into the darkness.

Did he see a ghost and talk to it?

Nervously aware of the canaller's disappearance and the brooding silence all about him, Jeppo hurriedly made his way back to the saloon.

He patted the bartender on the sleeve and announced, "Tonight, I for one have bottomed the depths of fear; now, fill my glass and let me drink my shot in peace." The liquor was strong, but it made him feel warm inside and that was what he needed.

"Nobody believes in spirits until something happens to them, and to tell the truth, neither did I," said Jeppo wiping his sleeve across his mouth.

The few customers still at the bar laughed and knew immediately that their friend, Jeppo, had at last met up with the "spirit" of Halloween.

It is alleged that on the stroke of midnight, on certain nights in the month of October, the phantom canaller and his boat have been seen traveling on the old canal system. Sometimes he stops for a brief spirited chat, but most of the time he waves his ghostly hand as he passes by the bridges. Still, to this day, not much is made of this momentary vision. It may be perfectly possible that he is one of the phantom-victims of those earlier canal days who feels compelled to remain earthbound to haunt the place of his death.

One thing remains certain . . . he is still being seen.

The Haunted Trailer

A couple of miles north of Port Byron is the well-landscaped trailer court where the King family found nothing but ghostly manifestations for many unhappy years.

Now a haunted house is one thing, it can be lived in. If there's a ghost wafting around, you can always lock yourself in another part of the house. But in a trailer . . . well, no way. Where can you go to get away from a "moving" ghost? This is the sort of a ghost story that is dear to my heart where witnesses abound and are very believable.

Early one morning my phone rang and a woman asked, "Are you the Johnson who wrote the book about ghosts in Port Byron?" Hesitantly I answered, "Yes." She laughed loudly and said, "Boy, am I glad you did, because now I know I'm not crazy!"

I immediately reached for a pen and pad. I knew a ghost story was about to be revealed.

"We lived in this town for over seven years and had a ghost haunting our trailer," she continued. "This ghost wafted across the trailer every night and would settle down on the sofa, usually with one long ectoplasmic arm resting near the end table. I thought I was going to faint the first time the misty figure came into view among the living room draperies. Then the figure suddenly headed toward me staring apprehensively into the darkness, and disappeared into the bathroom. We made a thorough search but found no one.

"Day and night we heard crashing noises. The sounds seemed to originate from the direction of the bathroom but nothing could be found to account for them.

"Some days we would return home from work and find the trailer in a complete shambles, articles thrown about and hardly anything in its right place. Unless our keys were in a zippered purse, they would disappear and be missing for several hours or overnight," Bernice complained.

"The trailer lights went on and off, television and radio both blared away while we were still at work. We would come and find the place in a party mood—music, ashtrays spilled onto the floor . . . and silverware found in the sink drainer after I had put them in the drawer."

Bernice's husband's rulers and tools would be missing one day, and the next all these articles would be strewn on the living room floor, always the living room.

Ghostly shadows walked the narrow hallway nightly and the smell of after-shave made life almost unbearable at times. The overpowering "Old Spice" fragrance was so suffocating that they had to open windows in the middle of the winter.

Groaning, frequently accompanied by heavy knocking, sometimes aroused the whole household. One night Bernice stood there in the shadowed hall listening to this groaning when a new ghostly sound flowed through the rooms. The sounds came from the bathroom. Upon investigations of these many eerie happenings, nothing could be found to explain them.

A fanning sensation, as though a bird was flying around, came from the living room from time to time. Bernice said they didn't even have a fan or air conditioner at the time. The sound of heavy breathing was heard and felt and an icy coldness usually preceded the manifestations.

Bernice was so upset that she finally reported it to the owner of the trailer park, but no one believed her and nothing was done about it.

In desperation, she finally called in a psychic from Syracuse who found that a spirit did live in the trailer, but he didn't know how to rid them of its presence.

The most terrifying incident was when the ghost came out of her husband's bedroom and walked to the bathroom, down the hallway and then to the living room. Bernice occupied the back bedroom and witnessed this strange happening. She immediately got out of bed and when she saw that her husband was asleep in his bed, ran down the hall to chase whatever was roaming around at that hour of the night. By then her husband joined in the search but found no one. Their car keys, which were on the coffee table, were missing. The car was still parked in the driveway. The keys were found the next morning, back on the table but not where they had left them.

The time Bernice's jewelry came up missing along with some other personal belongings, she resolved to make a systematic examination of the trailer at once, but found nothing. There can be no doubt that the frightening experiences at their trailer home so terrified the family that they had to move out of town.

I asked Bernice if they had any plans to move back there someday? "Never! And remember, don't give out my new address in your next ghost book," she added.

"Do you know, sometimes on still, quiet evenings, I almost get a creepy feeling that they (the ghosts) will walk in through the living room window and . . ." She broke off with a little shudder, then said, "Only time will tell."

The Blessed Virgin

As Therese lay dying in the hospital, she suddenly began to smile, her sister was standing near her bedside watching her. It was unbelievable—Therese was acting like herself again. She seemed exceedingly happy and without pain for a few moments.

Marie asked, "Therese, why are you smiling? Is there someone in that chair or do you see something we cannot see?" Standing by Marie was another dear friend whom Therese loved dearly. Therese nodded her head and whispered, "Yes," Marie looked over at the empty chair but could see nothing. Then she asked Therese, "Do you see God?" Therese shook her head and whispered, "No."

Marie then asked, "Is it the Blessed Virgin?"

Therese smiled and again nodded her head up and down, but didn't say anything to Marie. Her eyes were focused on the invisible image she was communicating with, nodding and smiling.

Marie was now completely convinced that Therese was indeed seeing the Mother of Jesus. She continued her questioning.

"Therese, does she have on a white dress?"

"No," she whispered and looked up at Marie and then away in the direction of the chair once again.

"Is it blue?" Marie asked. The reply was "Yes," and Therese smiled for the last time.

Therese died and her smile remained on her lips.

Castle Creek Mystery

In 1984, Alex and his wife Anne were living in a trailer near the town of Castle Creek.

Anne, a nurse, was working the late night shift at the VA hospital, and Alex was home with his dog Juniper.

It was around 11:30 on New Year's Eve. Juniper began acting very strangely and Alex became a little nervous. This was rather a wild countryside and his neighbors were miles away. Not to let his imagination run away with him, he decided to play some music on his new stereo before bedtime.

Juniper began to growl and then started barking near the trailer door. Alex opened the door very carefully to let the dog out but he wouldn't go. It was then that Alex heard the crying . . . it sounded like a young girl. He rushed back to the bedroom and put his clothes on. Soon screams and loud crying could be heard all around his trailer.

He took his pistol from its holster, put on his winter jacket and started for the door. He tried to get the dog to follow him outside, but he refused and continued his loud barking standing at the front door.

As Alex walked slowly around the yard, he was scared and afraid that the girl was being murdered . . . her screams and cries filled the cold night air.

He continued to search for her but couldn't see anyone, yet he felt she was close by. Her hysterical cries for help seemed to be coming from the nearby pond. He rushed in that direction. Her voice seemed louder and he knew he was getting closer. He could hear, "Help, please, help me." It was loud and clear and now seemed to be coming from near his garden.

He rushed toward that area and saw a young woman standing in a blue haze in the middle of his field. She seemed to be floating above the ground slightly. Her screams became softer and her hysterical voice seemed to be fading away, but the figure remained there in the mist.

He took his pistol and aimed it toward the garden and slowly approached the young girl, convinced there was someone there besides her. But as he drew closer to the blue haze spectral, she suddenly disappeared. No more screaming for help, no blue haze.

He returned to his trailer and immediately called his wife, who was still at the hospital. He told her the story, and she agreed with him that some investigation should be conducted immediately, but that they should wait for daylight.

Alex spent the rest of the night in the brilliantly lighted trailer, nervously going over in his mind what he should do next.

When he told his neighbors the frightening story, they knew what he had experienced because many of them had seen this young girl standing by a grave screaming and calling for help and always on New Year's Eve. But Alex didn't believe in any such ghostly tales and went to the proper authorities and asked if any murders had been committed recently. Nothing on record for this past New Year's Eve, he was told.

Anne remembered that this area was noted for its many ghost stories and that everyone tells the stories to an elderly lady, a former school teacher, who has kept a record of these sightings. Alex and Anne paid her a visit and when she heard the story she just lowered her head and said, "Yes, you have seen her. It is a sad story, but it is true."

Back in 1898 this young girl, her little brother and their parents drowned in the nearby pond on their way home from a house party on New Year's Eve. This apparition has been seen for many, many years; the young girl is earth bound in search of someone to help her and her family.

The Ghosts of Fayette

Millie asked, "How come you never write any ghost stories about Seneca Falls and Fayette?"

I replied, "Well, your mother-in-law told me stories about eerie incidents but they all happened when she was a young girl living with her parents in Port Byron. I have nothing on Fayette."

"My husband, Louie, has one scary tale," she said and called out to him. "Lou, come here and tell that haunted house story."

When Louie came into the room, he began his story. "In the heart of Seneca County and only a mile from Fayette, on the stretch of land that has remained unchanged since the days of

Brigham Young and the Mormons, there stands an isolated collection of buildings. They are grouped around an imposing farmhouse once owned by a local family whose name I have decided to keep out of the story to allow privacy to the new generation of their children still living in that area.

"When the old farmer died, he left his money to one of his sons, and the farm to the other. But the son who inherited the house refused to live in it and rented it out to the a family. They stayed there over many years but didn't like the hauntings that went on day and night."

One of the older children told Lou that the doors would lock without anyone near them. The pump handle would move up and down by itself in the middle of the night, pouring water all over the concrete slab of the deep well. During the winter months when the pump would freeze, the ghost had no trouble pumping water all over the yard.

The mother would be frightened out of a deep sleep every Monday washday morning around five a.m. when the old washing machine on the back porch would start washing away. Sometimes it had clothes in it and other times it was empty. Once she found the machine out under a tree and some invisible body was wringing clothes. Upon investigation, they found nothing but the old washer and a few dirty socks near it, but the nearby clothes line had clothes strung on it which they could not identify. There were strange looking pants and shirts as if from another time.

Lou said the old house has been empty for years now, but some say it is still haunted.

A recent visitor there had a terrifying experience. He decided to drive down the long, lonely driveway to check out the rumors. As the car was half way to the haunted house, it suddenly went into the ditch, over a bank, back on the road and into a mud puddle. It stalled and he couldn't get it started. Then the horn started blowing and his lights flickered on and off. Panic stricken, he jumped out of the car and ran for help. When he told the gas station attendant this spooky story, he refused to tow the car back to the main road. Several days later, with another garageman from Geneva, he was able to get his car going again.

Several years later another ghost incident came to my attention.

It was Halloween night and a car full of teenagers from Fayette decided to drive down to the haunted house. It was about the same location as other would-be ghost hunters had had trouble with their cars. They found the place eerie and heard noises coming from the dark, empty buildings and ran for help. As they rushed up the dirt road, Mary fell and scratched her knee, ripped a hole in her jeans and was hurting quite badly, but being more afraid than hurt, she lead the girls out of that haunted farm.

When Mary reached home, she looked down at her leg and saw there were deep cuts but she wasn't bleeding. Her family gathered around her and yelled, "Mary, those cuts look like initials . . . W.H." . . . the same as the former owner of this haunted house. Mary refused to ever discuss this incident until today when the family reunion relatives coaxed her into it. She doesn't believe in ghosts, but she is scared stiff of that old place.

Half Ghost

The housekeeper had just finished pressing the church linens and entered the living room to rest and say her prayers. It was by design, an eerie and uncomfortable room whose atmosphere invited its visitors to speak in whispers.

Glancing up at her dead sister's photograph which was positioned at an angle for easy viewing, she sobbed almost soundlessly. She had resigned herself to the fact that she would never see her again or hear her playing the piano.

Toward evening, although there was no light, she saw an unmistakable glimmer in the middle of the room which, as she watched, increased to a bright whiteness. To her amazement, she saw a beautiful white skirt, silently gliding toward the piano. It stopped, but she couldn't see anything from the waist up on the figure.

The housekeeper was stunned; was it her dead sister? For a while she could do nothing but stare in bewilderment at the skirt and dark shoes. When describing the clothing, she said afterwards that she could distinguish every fold in the full skirt.

Then came a sound like the sighing of a tired person. It is interesting to note that as well as being only partially visible and indistinct, the sighing of the spirit was very human.

As far as I know, her sister's apparition has not been seen again. It is thought that the mysterious half figure that the church woman claimed to have seen, may well have been her sister's ghost revisiting her home and piano.

I asked her if she was frightened. "Frightened? No, I wasn't frightened! I was trying to think of a likely explanation." She seemed to have suffered no ill effects from her experience —instead she was rather proud of it.

How often are we visited by the spirit of a loved one?

Ghostly Flour Prints

The century and a half old grocery-bakery store made news in the early 1900s when noises and a small ghost child pestered the owner and the customers. According to reliable reports, it continues to this very day.

The young "form" seems to appear regularly every month or so. The current occupants are aware of its presence because it makes mysterious noises and shakes flour on the floor, leaving small footprints as it goes to its haunted storeroom in the back of the bakery. Fingerprints are always found on the floured countertop.

Once the owner was shocked to see a young child standing near the counter. When she spoke to him, he seemed to pass clear through the glass showcase. At first the owner was skeptical, but after hearing first hand evidence from customers and friends, changed her views and knew now that what she was seeing was indeed a ghost.

Sometimes the creak of a chair is heard, a soft sigh follows, then the ghost approaches the counter where the owner is preparing her baked goods. A peculiar chill is often noticed when the ghost is present. Articles are moved and even strewn about, if the owner leaves the room.

One of the family members stated that he entered the room in the company of five other people and they all observed the ghost walking around the counter. He said the form was making no sound.

The owner cannot find any record of a child's death in her building. Gradually this family has learned to live with their ghostly child. The small store located in Auburn remains haunted by this small entity.

Quite recently they reported seeing the white ghost child figure coming towards them as they worked in the bakery. When the form had nearly reached the doorway to the dimly-lit back room, it vanished.

This store has many secrets and one lonely little ghost child.

The Nun

"This is about a very old nun. Even though it's been many years, we'd know her if we met her today," Aunt Jane and Uncle Rocky told their niece Ann. It was at their fiftieth wedding anniversary party that this eerie story was told.

"We were driving along the side roads one afternoon around dusk, when we saw a nun walking along the shoulder. The nun heard our car coming and flagged us down. She asked if we would drive her to the nearby cemetery. Nuns walking along a road were considered something of an oddity in those days. She was dressed in her habit that was dark and worn looking."

Aunt Jane said she wasn't able to clearly make out the features of her face for her head was draped with a loose shroud-like piece of material. Something about her expression made me think of a shy person, yet there was a self-assured, friendly air about the nun which made Rocky relax even though he didn't like the idea of picking up strange hitchhikers, even in a nun's habit!

"Her skirts brushed Jane as she turned and entered the back seat of our car. I remember she paused before the door and gave us a warm broad smile, but she seemed to be giving off very cold air." Jane and Rocky did their best to ignore this sensation. "The nun settled herself near the back window with a small watering pail resting on her lap. It was then I noticed the pail had holes in the bottom of it."

"I have never had the shadow of a doubt about having a real live nun in our car; we never thought of her as a phenomenon. There was nothing misty or ghost-like about her body either.

"When we reached the cemetery, the nun thanked us and slowly walked to the heavy iron gates at the entrance. We didn't see her open them but she was inside when she waved us to go on. Rocky decided to wait there for a few minutes to make sure she didn't need a ride back. He complained it was a helluva way to spend his day off . . . waiting at a strange cemetery for a mysterious old nun!" The last glimpse they saw was the nun standing on the lawn of a grave, her habit billowing and snapping in the wind, and the pail swinging from her small, bony hand. They were puzzled at this strange sight, then the nun seemed to vanish behind a gravestone.

"We thought about that experience a lot," Rocky said. "The next part sounds funny, but we didn't know what else to do so we invited our friends to the spot where the nun had waved us down for a ride. As a rule my memory about where and when I left the old nun is excellent, but for the life of me, I could not find that cemetery. And to this day there isn't any trace of a cemetery ever being on this Auburn road."

Neither Rocky nor Jane had ever seen an apparition before that day, nor have they since. That nun wasn't in the least bit like a ghost and the thought never even crossed their minds until several days later when they could not locate the cemetery. One thing they do remember about the old nun is that as soon as their eyes met hers, she would turn her head away much faster than they thought humanly possible.

Rocky said, "I've thought about that experience a lot since

114

then. No matter what anyone says, I now have no doubt about a world beyond."

Feathers

If tragic deaths and violent happenings can cause hauntings, then the old hogan should be ghost-ridden.

Bari, who worked on a cattle ranch in this area, heard the lonely cries of coyotes nightly and enjoyed their moonlight harmony. That is until the ghostly story of Zuker came into her life.

It is known that some cowboys love to pass the time away playing cards and sometimes for higher stakes than they can afford. It was payday and after such an evening of gambling, cowboy Zuker and friends headed for their ranch house. Somewhere between the River Saloon and the hogan (Indian meeting house), Zuker was killed. He was accused of cheating at cards. The murder was never solved, and to this very day the town is divided as to his guilt or innocence.

Zuker's ghost has appeared to many as they traveled this lonely country road. It is told that before his untimely death, he always met his dearly beloved at the hogan and that is where his ghost is often seen. Sometimes standing near the old entrance, other times leaning against the well pump, holding a deck of cards in one hand and his Colt .45 in the other.

It was some time before Bari met up with her friend, Feathers, and the Zuker story was the first thing she intended to greet her with, but knowing Feathers, she gave her a rundown on ranch life instead. Three days went by until Bari had the nerve to mention ghostly Zuker. Of course Feathers didn't believe a word of it and challenged Bari and her friends to a Ouija board seance at the hogan to prove her point. It wouldn't take very long, all they had to do was contact Zuker. And that they did . . . Zuker cooperated beyond her belief . . . he told them he did not cheat at cards.

Feathers only half believed the ghost story now. A few nights later as she strolled by the hogan, she was surprised to see a handsome cowboy dressed in a buckskin jacket and jeans leaning against the doorway. As she slowly approached him, he disappeared into the wall behind him. Feathers screamed . . . "It's Zuker."

The sightings continued to plague Feathers; nightly disturbances began occurring in her home and became increasingly frightening. A black-grayish, flimsy shapeless glob would appear at the outer door of her ranch house; vibrations from the armoire, which was made from planks of gallows, nearly drove her insane. It haunted her thoughts by day, her slumber by night. She soon became haggard and despondent.

Things really got out of hand when Feathers saw ghostly Zuker standing at the foot of her iron bed. He seemed to be human in shape but his eyes were like two black holes in his face. The most objectionable part of the experience was the accompanying smell, a most appalling stench, such as one would expect from a decaying corpse. After a moment the figure and the odor vanished as inexplicably as they had arrived. It was a long time before Feathers recovered from the shock.

When she couldn't get ghostly Zuker out of her mind, and on the advice of her family and friends, Feathers decided the best cure was a change of scenery. She joined a convent in Mexico, where she became a devout Catholic.

Ghostly Zuker left shortly afterwards and never returned to Feathers or the hogan. To this very day, Feathers believes that the Holy Spirit at last granted Zuker passage into the other world.

Sweet Hauntings

It was inevitable, of course, but why did it have to happened to me? Bari was the first person in our family to live in a haunted house with my grandmother, Sophia. I wasn't married but was unemployed at the time and Gram needed help. That's why.

Lightning strikes my grandmother's house many times each summer and when I was a young child, I was not allowed to use the telephone during a thunderstorm. As my dad tells it, Grandmother was about to talk on the phone when a bolt of lightning struck her and hurled her to the floor and the whole room glowed in the blue light of St. Elmo's fire. Grandmother too!

Soon after that frightening incident, Grandmother began talking to the ghosts in residence. She explained to Bari that she didn't mind that her house was haunted. In fact she rather enjoyed arguing with her ghostly friends whenever things became too noisy. It was the disappearance of food from her pantry that upset her. Every morning she would find her favorite banana bread, cookies and other desserts scattered all over the kitchen. This was a ghost who ate nothing but sweets, Sophia would declare to all as she hustled about trying to clean up the mess. At one point, she thought seriously of shooting her two tomcats because they refused to go into the kitchen after dark. Sophia knew then and there that it wasn't mice getting into her desserts, but ghosts. Animals have a keen sense of smell and know when they are about.

Bari said, "It might be appropriate to mention some of the other manifestations that have been noticed at Grandmother's place."

In the main living room off the hallway, card shuffling could be heard almost every night after supper. At times the old rocking chair would rock until the cushions fell onto the Persian rug. One evening, Sophia had had about enough of these ghostly tricks and threw the deck of cards to the floor and went to bed. Suddenly she felt someone yanking on the bed covers. She sat up and ordered the ghosts to stop all these nightly disturbances or else she and her family would be moving out. To her surprise, all the ghostly manifestations stopped.

A Night to Remember

"What was the thing you've done that scared you the most?" I asked Rita. "I won't tell you that, but I'll tell you the worst thing that ever happened to me—the most frightening," she answered in her young voice.

"At some time everyone has been frightened of something they've heard but not seen; a creaking floorboard or doors opening and closing without the help of a person, but I see things happening all around me," Rita explained.

She and her family have lived in the same lovely home on Seymour Street for many years and have had to live with disturbances from spirits.

"I've heard a number of ghost stories about Auburn homes," she said, "but I've never heard of anything this bad occurring in any other house. My greatest fear was that this utterly terrifying malevolent force would try to harm one of my children or someone visiting us.

"The latest incident happened only a few months ago. It was close to midnight, when I heard knockings on the side of the living room walls. I tried to locate the sound but as soon as I approached the walls, the noise stopped. After a few hours of such rappings, I checked the backyard and found blood here and there but no trace of a wounded animal or evidence of any struggle. Just spots of blood, some very close to our back door. Usually after such sightings, I hear knockings on the cellar door—the inside door leading upstairs to the kitchen. Sometimes when I am home alone, the door opens but no one enters. A strange feeling of someone watching me from the stairwell makes me shiver.

"It keeps me up all night, as the following morning will bring even more trouble. The cellar is always in shambles, cans of food strewn all over the concrete floor, cigarette butts crushed here and there on my furniture and shelves. No one in my family smokes. I can never find any smoke smell or ashes, just butts and tobacco everywhere but in the ash can."

Rita believes something disastrous must have happened outside her home a long time ago and the spirit of this tragic incident remains on her property. Believers say the spirit is earthbound until this mystery is solved.

One thing is for sure, Rita says, even the police haven't been able to solve this case.

Shapeshifting

Angelo admits he did see his beloved Lenora again and she appeared as a black leopard sitting on her front porch swing.

"Shapeshifting" appears in the folklore of all people. These beings have been talked about in folk history for thousands of years. The studies made of shapeshifting foxes, wolves, dogs, etc. are probably sound, but most believe shapeshifting in folklore is clearly connected with hallucination. Until more studies are done, we are not able to go beyond the general observation that nothing is what it seems to be. These beings can convince you that you are losing your mind. Such things can not happen!

But we do see them and they do happen!

Angelo said that Lenora came from nowhere. There is no record of her in the town she said she was born and lived in until she moved to his town. "Of course there couldn't be," Angelo said, "because there was never such a town."

She was a ghost who could be dangerous and yet very witty. She loved playing jokes on Angelo. He said her feet never touched the path they usually took on their walks together. Sometimes she would appear to be floating ten or more inches above the ground. Did Angelo imagine this? He thought he was going to faint the first time it happened.

When describing his Lenora, all he could say was that she was "gypsyish, with curly black hair fluffing out around a sensual young face. She had well-shaped arms and beautiful long legs," Angelo fell in love with her soon after their first meeting in the church graveyard. "Well, I'm here, come and get me," he said to Lenora and smiled. She did and they were together for years.

One October afternoon, he deliberately set off on what was normally his return path and found leopard footprints imprinted in the new fallen snow. It was not the cold that kept Angelo moving briskly, but nervousness that some unforeseen happening might prevent Lenora from meeting him. Above him the sky was scattered with dark, stormy clouds. Suddenly the same black leopard he had seen on Lenora's swing earlier that day came leaping at him. It stopped short of his chest and stared at him with a calm, expressionless gaze and a grim face. He felt an utter terror and quickly covered his face with his hands. When he removed them and could see again, the leopard was gone.

Lenora was never seen again and Angelo died shortly after this frightening incident from a broken heart.

Today, when the townspeople hear the cries of a lonely leopard late at night, they whisper, "Is that Lenora looking for her dear Angelo?"

A Short Ghost Story

Dear Mary Ann,

Glad to hear about your ghost book. When do you get time to write?

Hope all goes well for you.

I have never seen a ghost. But when I was a teenager, I was babysitting for this young girl. A person appeared at the bottom of the bed. We were sleeping in twin beds. It seems like it was a man with a turban on his head and puffy pants and pointed turned-up shoes. As soon as I got up he ran down the cellar stairs.

I can still remember it. I didn't tell her parents, but needless to say I never babysat for her again.

Love,
Doris

120